DOCTORS, LAWYERS, MINISTERS:

DOCTORS, LAWYERS, MINISTERS:

CHRISTIAN ETHICS IN PROFESSIONAL PRACTICE

DENNIS M. CAMPBELL

Abingdon
NASHVILLE

DOCTORS, LAWYERS, MINISTERS:
CHRISTIAN ETHICS IN PROFESSIONAL PRACTICE

Copyright © 1982 by Abingdon

Library of Congress Cataloging in Publication Data
CAMPBELL, DENNIS M., 1945–
  Doctors, lawyers, ministers.
  Bibliography: p.
  Includes index.
  1. Professional ethics.   2. Christian ethics—
Methodist authors.   I. Title.
BJ1725.C35   241'.64   82-4049   AACR2

ISBN 0-687-11016-5

Scripture quotations unless otherwise noted are from the Revised Standard
Version of the Bible, copyright 1946, 1952, 1971, © 1973, by the Division of
Christian Education of the National Council of the Churches of Christ in the
U.S.A., and used by permission.

MANUFACTURED BY THE PARTHENON PRESS AT
NASHVILLE, TENNESSEE, UNITED STATES OF AMERICA

CONTENTS

PREFACE

This book is an essay in applied Christian theology. Theology best comes to life when persons see that it makes a difference in the church community. One's theological understanding shapes one's life. Theology and ethics, therefore, go together in Christian thought.

My research, teaching, and reflection in theology, ethics, and the professions have spanned a number of years since my first exposure to some of the issues this book addresses. From 1968 to 1970, I was privileged to work with a team of persons based at Yale Divinity School gathered by the late Kenneth W. Underwood. This group assisted with a study sponsored by the Danforth Foundation which resulted in two volumes entitled *The Church, the University and Social Policy*. That study was concerned in part with the professions and professional education; and it started me thinking about the relationship of Christian theology to the professions.

My experience as a minister in parish churches brought me into close contact with professionals who seek some integration of their Christian faith with their professional practice. I became convinced that the church needs to understand and speak more effectively to the settings in which its members spend their lives. Later, as a professor of religion teaching undergraduates, I found students asking questions about the relationship of religion to everyday life.

The initial funds that allowed me to undertake this project came from a Faculty Research Council Grant received in 1978 from Converse College. Among the things it made possible was an opportunity to work at the Institute of Society, Ethics, and the Life Sciences at Hastings-on-Hudson, New York. I received a warm welcome and experienced the spirit of collegiality which has come to characterize that important research center.

The specific impetus for this book came as a result of an invitation to give four lectures to a national meeting of physicians and clergy in the fall of 1978. Clarence C. Lyles, a pediatrician who understands his professional practice to be an expression of his profession of faith, was responsible for that invitation and has helped me think about the complex realities professionals face in modern American society.

This book has gained much from the support and advice of numerous students and colleagues at Converse College, Duke University, and other institutions, where sections have been given as lectures, as well as from colleagues in the ministry. I acknowledge gladly and gratefully the help of the staffs of William R. Perkins Library, the Duke Law School Library, and the Duke Medical School Library. For special assistance, I am indebted to James Harrison, director of Gwathmey Library at Converse and to Donn Michael Farris, librarian, and Harriet V. Leonard, reference librarian, at the Duke Divinity School Library.

Patsy Martin and Candice Sloan have contributed greatly to this project; their marvelous attitudes and exceptional skills aid all my work.

My wife, Leesa, whose own theological education makes her my best initial critic, and my children, Margaret and Trevor, have shared with this book hours that perhaps rightly should have been theirs.

The book is dedicated to my parents, F. M. and Margaret Campbell; their faithfulness, love, and support got me started on the way.

—D. M. C.

INTRODUCTION

The traditional professions in American society are in a state of crisis. Public attitudes no longer regard them with unqualified admiration. Current practitioners find conditions changed from when they entered the profession, and are uncertain about the future. Professional education is being challenged from within and without; alternative curricula and proposals for new models of professional education concern both educators and practitioners. As institutions of a complex and rapidly changing society, it should not surprise us that professions reflect, even as they are called to give guidance to, the society. Change, even when it is good change, is unsettling and requires significant new thinking. How the professions will deal with the opportunities and problems now before them is a topic of pressing concern.

Whenever consideration of the professions begins, the matter of ethics comes to the fore. This is so, no doubt, because ethics has always been a concern of the professions; but it is also the case that ethics has become a concern as a result of the very factors that have brought the professions to crisis: popular perception, whether fairly or unfairly, often views the professions as bastions of power and privilege inordinately concerned to maintain and perpetuate themselves.

There is an ever-growing literature on ethics and medicine, biomedical ethics, and to a lesser extent, legal

ethics. Relatively little material is being published that
seeks to examine the professions as institutions of American
society and that seeks to explore the ethical issues involved
in the way in which the professions as institutions operate in
the society. Not long ago, I lectured to a group of
physicians. When I finished, a pediatric surgeon told me
that he never knew before why medicine was called a
profession. He further suggested that he always thought of
ethics as a very personal matter and never considered that
ethical decision making might be informed, or even
judged, from criteria external to his own conscience or
"feelings." The idea that the impact of the medical
profession *as a whole* was *itself* an ethical issue, he said, was
an entirely new idea.

I became interested in ethics and the professions for two
reasons. The first is that for a number of years I have been
concerned about professional education and the nature of
the formation that takes place in a professional school.
There is a growing recognition among men and women
who are engaged in teaching future professionals that
problems and issues in professional practice overlap. This is
evident whenever a case-study approach is used among
future or practicing professionals. Regardless of specialization, the ethical problems are the same and must be dealt
with from a variety of perspectives. Moreover, it is
increasingly evident that better education in ethical
reflection needs to be provided as a part of the professional
school curriculum.

Second, my experience in teaching undergraduate
liberal arts students who are preparing for entry into
professional education convinced me that the process of
education for ethical decision making should be a part of
the undergraduate curriculum. Undergraduate liberal arts

courses can be structured so that value considerations can be explored and decision making practiced in a setting less highly charged than professional school course work.

My interest in ethics and the professions led to the development of a course designed for preprofessional students. We examined the history of the professions and their current state and future shape. We explored ways of ethical reasoning and worked with case studies which illumined the interdisciplinary nature of moral decisions. We talked about professional education and the nature and purpose of professional schools. I received a grant for a series of lectures designed to bring professional educators and practitioners to the campus. The undergraduate response was enthusiastic. Professional ethics is a topic not only of great importance, but also of wide interest. This wide interest is further exemplified by the fact that professional organizations are giving attention to the topic in conferences and publications.

This story leads to the reason for this book. My research and lecturing forced me to ask myself, Why am I, a Christian theologian, spending so much time on ethics and the professions? This led me to the further question, What can I contribute that is helpful? In reflecting on these two questions, I came to several conclusions:

1. It seems to me that serious attention needs to be given to the important matter of the ethical implications of the professions as institutions of American society.

2. Because American society today is pluralist, much of what has been done in professional ethics avoids specific religious content or reference. Scholars who work in the field of religious ethics have much to contribute which is not predicated upon prior commitment to a given religious tradition. That is, it is possible to address a group of

professionals and talk about ethics without appealing to religious reasoning. In working with the house staff in a teaching hospital, or a bar association one cannot assume religious homogeneity. Significant work in professional ethics has been done from the point of view of philosophical analysis. It seems to me, however, that there is a legitimate place for specific reflection on the relationship between Christian faith and professional ethics.

3. The issues in professional ethics are complex and the disciplines of philosophical and religious ethics are sophisticated. It is difficult to get an overview of the issues. It seems to me that there is a need for an approach that can offer some helpful insight into the complexities of ethics and the professions for the general reader, the practitioner, and the student.

4. In all the professions, significant numbers of serious Christians are seeking a relationship between their Christian faith and their professional practice. Christian teaching has always proposed that faith manifests itself in the believer's daily life; and the church has emphasized the necessity of understanding one's work as Christian service. The problem of making this idea a reality is not easy. The professions have grown to be complex institutions in modern society. This increased complexity has made it seem even more difficult to find relationships between daily work in practice and Christian faith. The images and ideas that professionals, and the lay public, have available when they think about the important issues of contemporary professional practice are not adequate in the face of new realities. Christian men and women need to work together to develop new ways of thinking about the implications of faith in daily life.

5. A major obligation of Christian theology today is to demonstrate convincingly that Christian faith can and does make a difference in people's lives. This requires systematic work in the development of the Christian tradition, in constructive theological thinking, and in reflection on the relationship between theology and the moral life. This book is also a theological proposal. A way of thinking theologically is set forth and is then tested for its applicability to the realities of complex modern life.

The plan of the book is to offer an overview of the idea of the professions and to demonstrate that an understanding of the development of the professions provides some normative principles by which practice can be judged. Chapters are devoted to theological analysis, to reflections on Christian moral formation, and to specific problems which unite pressing issues for the law, for medicine, and for ministry. The case studies are designed to demonstrate the interprofessional character of so many contemporary problems.

This book is intended not only for men and women who are currently engaged in the professional disciplines directly related to the subject, but also for undergraduates who are thinking about professional education, for students currently confronting the challenges of professional education, and for the general reader who recognizes that the contemporary crisis in the professions has grave implications for American society. The book is written to spark discussion and further reflection and is in no sense definitive. If I can provide some ways to help men and women better understand Christian faith and its relation to professional practice, I will have achieved my purpose in writing. My conviction is that Christian thinking can illumine the problems of the professions, and that attention to these problems is essential.

THE IDEA OF PROFESSION:

FOUNDATIONS AND ETHICAL IMPLICATIONS

1

THE NATURE OF A PROFESSION

The Traditional Definition

The word "profession" is used in popular culture to refer to all kinds of occupations. One encounters advertisements celebrating the quality of services rendered by "professional" insurance salespeople, "professional" hair stylers, and "professional" exterminators. Routinely we talk about "professional" athletes and "professional" military officers. These usages are intended to suggest full-time involvement in a given occupation from which one earns a living and a certain quality that characterizes the performance of that occupation. The word "professional" is chosen to evoke an aura of respect and to elicit from those who are not professionals a confidence in the one performing the service or fulfilling the role.

Sociologists have written extensively on the professions.[1] One of the areas of study in sociological literature concerns the definition of a profession.[2] It is quite clear that any number of occupations have consciously, or sometimes unconsciously, sought to improve their standards and expectations by seeking to conform to some of the traditional notions of what being a professional means.[3] It is not the intention of this book to participate in the lively and important discussions of the sociology of the professions, nor is it my intention to challenge those who, for often noble reasons, seek to claim the title "professional." It is, however, necessary for me to define what I mean by the term "profession" and to explain what this book will and will not propose to discuss.

Some confusion exists about the proper use of the word "professional"; but the use of the English language is not regulated by any agency with authority. It is, therefore, pointless to spend much time debating the use of a word. The fact that the word is used, however, in an effort to lend increased status to an occupation, indicates that the word carries with it connotations of quality; that is, status as a professional is to be sought, not to be shunned. Regardless of contemporary usage, it is possible to set forth a traditional definition of a professional. The traditional definition is particularly important to this study because it is the starting point for any consideration of ethics and the professions.

The earliest use of the word "profession" was in relation to religious orders. "To profess" was to take upon oneself the vows of a religious order. This usage of the word developed in the thirteenth and fourteenth centuries in Europe, especially in Italy and England, and came to refer to orders of monks and nuns. The story of the growth and development of the religious orders in medieval Europe is fascinating. Supported by laity who believed that monks and nuns were performing essential services on behalf of all people, they were an outlet for penitential giving. The orders also provided a place where sons, who were not the first-born, and daughters, who, for whatever reason, could not be suitably matched in marriage, could find an acceptable way of life. The religious communities were a major institution in medieval society. They were, in fact, international institutions which transcended local customs and advanced Christian civilization throughout the Western world.

Perhaps most significantly, monasteries and nunneries became the centers of culture and education. Art and learning were protected and encouraged; and interest in learning was fused with a commitment to service. The cultural synthesis which was championed by the medieval Roman Catholic Church united what we might now call the sacred and secular realms of experience. All society was properly under the purview of the church. This synthesis allowed "religious professionals" to take a lively interest in a wide range of activities which were not specifically "religious." Thus the religious orders provided society with artists, educators, experts in law, men and women who served the sick, and political advisors and leaders, as well as theologians, priests, and ministers.

Members of religious orders, or "religious professionals," provided these varied services because few others could provide them. The structure of medieval society was such that a secular, professional middle-class did not exist. Moreover, people of the Middle Ages were self-consciously religious and understood themselves, and their world, in Christian categories. Perhaps the most difficult thing for twentieth-century men and women to understand is that medieval people *really believed* in a traditional Christian explanation of the world. Education, therefore, was under the auspices of the church; and the development of the universities was a function of certain houses of religious orders. The medieval university was one major work of "religious professionals" and, in the university context, expertise was developed in various "disciplines," but especially in divinity, law, and medicine.

The expertise required of the "religious professionals" who specialized in law, medicine, and divinity grew in the university context. Their university base distinguished them from the guilds which were technical vocations. In England, for instance, surgeons were regarded as technicians and were members of a guild rather than a profession because, as technicians, they were not based in a university. Barbers and surgeons, being variously skilled with scalpels or razors, were one guild. To this day, in England, surgeons are addressed as "mister," the designation "doctor" being studiously avoided. A quirk of history has thus become an occasion for reverse snobbishness.

Gradually the vocations of law, medicine, and divinity came to be regarded as unique professions. Often these professionals were clergy, and almost all students were required to take at least minor clerical orders; but by the sixteenth century, at least, the word "profession" was being applied to men who, though not ordained, practiced these disciplines. It is impossible to provide a precise description of the gradual development of the non-clerical (that is, non-ordained) professions. Clearly by the late Middle Ages, physicians and lawyers who had made no formal acceptance of the religious state were practicing. This is not to say, of course, that these professions were divorced from the church. Such an assumption would fail to comprehend the medieval synthesis, already described, which understood all vocations in a Christian context. Although the traditional learned professions did not remain exclusively clerical, their roots in the religious orders decidedly shaped the way they were conceived and practiced. The use of the term "laity" to refer to those untrained in any one of the professions is indicative of their clerical foundations. Originally the term "laity" was used to distinguish ordinary people from the clergy; it came to refer to those not belonging to a profession.[4]

The three traditional learned professions are divinity,

law, and medicine. In addition to these three, late medieval society tended to view the military as a profession.[5] Perhaps this was so because military service involved the swearing of loyalty to one's superior, whether he were a lord, a prince, or a king. Perhaps, too, the military man was regarded as a professional because of the expectation that he commit himself to service of the church. The idea of the "Christian warrior" elevated the status of the military. The military was always set apart from the learned professions, however, because it was different. It did not conform to the expectations that characterized law, medicine, and theology. It is possible to identify the characteristics that became normative to the concept of what it means to be a professional:

1. The professional is engaged in a *social service* that is *essential and unique.* A profession is recognized by society as performing an identifiable and necessary service which cannot be performed by one who is not a member of the profession. We know that for certain services we need trained professionals. Should one have medical problems, one sees a physician. Only lawyers practice law. This first point is simple, but important. The service a professional renders is readily identifiable.

2. The professional is one who has developed a *high degree of knowledge.* The professions require intellectual skills of a high order. Usually professional knowledge presupposes a liberal background in the arts and sciences. This tradition is rooted in the sound medieval tradition that there is a body of knowledge that is shared by educated persons. The ancient and honorable degree of bachelor of arts signifies acceptance into the company of those who have been trained in a common body of knowledge.

Upon completion of the baccalaureate degree, the

professional student enters into a number of years of advanced training designed to develop competence in the systematic body of particular knowledge that informs and is prescribed by the profession. This period of advanced training is done in a professional school. Faculty members are practitioners of the given profession as well as scholars in their disciplines. The number of years of post-baccalaureate training varies, but for law, medicine, and divinity, the professional degree is ordinarily earned in three or four years.

3. The professional must develop the *ability to apply the special body of knowledge* that is unique to the profession. Professionals are men and women who are able to make their special knowledge useful to the society. Theory must be brought to bear on issues of common concern to people. Professional men and women do not stand aloof from the exigencies of life.

Professional school faculty members need experience in the practice of the profession so that they can bring their disciplinary expertise to bear on the problems their students will face. Moreover, professional students need to learn from those who are currently full-time practitioners. Various methods of internship are used in the professions to allow the student to achieve immediate experience under the guidance of a seasoned practitioner. The knowledge gained by a professional is knowledge that must be applied in service to the society. This skilled application of carefully developed knowledge is as old as the idea of profession itself, being firmly rooted in the effort to combine knowledge and service on the part of the members of medieval religious orders.

4. The professional is part of a group that is *autonomous and claims the right to regulate itself*. Only those who have demonstrated the necessary intellectual skills, liberal

background in the arts and sciences, competence in the particular knowledge requisite of the profession, as well as the refined skills of application, are admitted to practice. Only those who already possess this knowledge and skill are competent to judge prospective professionals. Similarly, only those who are already engaged in professional practice, it is argued, are capable of evaluating their peers. Every profession thus develops methods of judging the way in which individuals within the profession are behaving. A disciplined style, about which judgments can be made, is central to the professional life. This is one of the most important characteristics of a profession.

The exclusive right to self-regulation means that the professions have autonomy and power. The idea of autonomy is rooted in the practice of the medieval guild which was self-governing and policed its own ranks. The fact that this characteristic of a profession has been criticized will concern us later in the book. At this point, it is important to understand that autonomy and self-regulation have always been fundamental to the professional ideal. The authority that derives from autonomy produces a rigid wall between the professionals and the laity they serve.

5. The professional recognizes and affirms a *code of ethics*. In some cases, the code is quite specific and identifiable, such as the Hippocratic Oath, the Code of Professional Responsibility of the American Bar Association, or particular codes pertaining to specialized practice. Codes are not as important, however, as a long tradition of concern for ethical practice within a profession. One of the marks of an occupation seeking to become more professional is the introduction of a code of ethics. One thinks, for instance, of associations of morticians. The reason for the introduction of such codes has to do with the

recognition that a genuine profession needs a deep and abiding concern for ethical practice.

The learned professions are experiencing trouble with traditional codes and practices in contemporary society. Ethical problems are complex and more subtle in a time of sophisticated technology and governmental intervention. The point to be made here is that a concern for ethics is one of the *defining* characteristics of a profession.

6. The professional exhibits a strong *self-discipline* and *accepts personal responsibility* for actions and decisions. A professional's self-discipline is developed through years of preparation within the profession. Each profession must socialize those who seek to join it. A disciplined style of behavior has been central to the professional life since the word was first used in relation to religious orders. Discipline is internalized during professional education and through associations maintained by the professions. Self-discipline has always been essential for the self-employed solo practitioner. But the fact that professionals have always practiced within organizations does not lessen the reality of the need for self-discipline. Self-discipline refers not only to the commitment of time and energy, but also to the discipline that is required for excellence.

Self-discipline is closely linked to the acceptance of personal responsibility for decisions made in practice. The true professional cannot be a functionary; accountability for both the procedures and results of his or her work is recognized and accepted.

7. The professional's primary concern and commitment is to *communal interest* rather than merely to the self. This means that the professional places neither his or her own self-interest, nor the self-interests of those who are served above a concern for the greater good of the entire society.

The professional is expected to think about the consequences of a given case in the larger context of a society's needs and interests. There will, on occasion, be conflict between the immediate needs or desires of a given individual who seeks help from a professional and the long-range needs of the community. To be a professional is to realize such conflicts, think about them, and accept responsibility for one's actions. Later in the book, I will discuss this problem at length, for it is a problem of increasing proportion. Professionals are dealing with growing numbers of cases in which communal needs and individual needs are in conflict.

8. The professional is more concerned with *services rendered* than with *financial rewards*. Professionals do not "work for wages"; money is not the reason they offer their services. Traditionally, the professional received an "honorarium," an offering which was to "honor" him for his services rather than to "pay" him for services rendered. To this day, for instance, the robes worn by an English barrister have a pocket in the back. Today the pocket is symbolic, a relic left over from the days when the barrister's clerk would slip the honorarium in the pocket after it was received from the client. The barrister himself did not deign to handle money. No set of charges was established by the professional; indeed often honoraria were determined according to the individual financial condition of the person who received the professional's services.

Even in a time when professionals are paid increasingly by salary, the notion of honoraria is not dead. Few professionals are "paid what they legitimately earn." "Legitimate earnings" are difficult to determine; and professional remuneration is still regarded as being of a different order from hourly wages, or even annual compensation. Professional men and women often receive large sums of money, but it is rare to find even the best-paid physicians or attorneys suggesting that they are professionals *in order* to make money. Many may, in fact, have chosen their occupation because professionals are well compensated; but the concept of occupation as profession nevertheless carries with it a sense of service. The idea that the professional is concerned primarily about the *quality* of his or her practice and not the ability to "make money" is still very much a characteristic of professional style.

"Style" is an appropriate word to describe the combination of attributes that distinguish the professional. Professional style brings together all the factors described above; and perhaps finally it is "style" that defines the professional.[6] Style makes the difference between work done as a profession and work done as a job. It emerges from practice in response to the necessary combination of intellectual skills and learning, and practical skills and application. One cannot be "taught" professional style, it must be "caught" in the process of professional education including internships with seasoned practitioners. When professional men and women evaluate one another, the quality they recognize and admire is style. Perhaps it is significant, too, that when nonprofessional people comment on professionals, it is often matters of style that receive attention. The realities of modern professional style appear to diverge from the traditional notion of what it means to be a professional. This divergence deserves exploration.

Contemporary Developments

The picture of the professional set forth in the traditional definition above is, of course, an ideal type. Many readers would reject the criteria as unrealistic. It will be useful to identify some of the contemporary developments concerning the nature of a profession. It seems to me that there are at least four major points to be considered when discussing the meaning of the professions today.

1. A widely held conviction in American society is that the professions fail even to approximate the ideals set forth in a traditional definition. Professional, for some, has come to suggest technical competence applied in what is often an insensitive way, and resulting in large sums of money for the practitioner. "Professional" means little more than the opposite of "lay" or "amateur." The "pro" is the one who has enough skill to make money doing something most people cannot do. It is not uncommon to find people for whom "professional" conjures up ideas of actual malevolence or greed.

Cynicism toward the professions is directed especially at law and medicine. The cynicism results from the conviction on the part of many people that there is a gap between what the profession purports to stand for and the realities of the situation. Once the word "professional" carried with it a connotation of service, but now for many it implies selfishness.

2. Despite the fact the professions seem to be distrusted in contemporary society, they remain high in status. Polls that ask Americans to rank occupations in order of prestige demonstrate that American people continue to recognize the traditional learned professions as high-status occupations.[7] The clergy, physicians, college and university professors, and lawyers command prestige, even if they are not given unqualified respect. The fact that the professions are, in general, well-compensated occupations is one major reason for their high status.

3. Because the traditional professions remain high in status, and despite the fact that there is a certain cynicism about the professions, an ever-increasing number of occupations are seeking professional status. Research sociologists call this process "professionalization."[8] It refers to the efforts of occupational groups to approximate the professional ideal and thus achieve higher status and the resultant benefits, not the least of which is better compensation. "Professionalization" involves the introduction of codes of ethics, increased expectations about education, procedures for accrediting individual practitioners, and the establishment of group norms and identity.

What is a profession and what is a semiprofession? Most people would readily accord professional status to the law, medicine, and divinity. But what about architecture, the military, politics, or journalism? College and university professors are usually recognized as professionals, although increasing unionization activities may jeopardize the status; and serious studies suggest that elementary and secondary schoolteachers are becoming deprofessionalized in American society.[9] Morticians and beauticians are examples of occupational groups that have sought to raise standards and adopt the term professional, but popular perception lags behind the claims of these groups. The fact that more and more groups are seeking professional identity has made it necessary for the traditional professions to evaluate their own identities.

4. The professions are becoming institutionalized and the meaning of professional practice is being changed. The traditional definition of a profession emphasizes the responsibility and freedom of the individual practitioner within the context of his or her profession. In the past few decades, it has become common for professionals to work

for institutions, corporations, or associations in which they are salaried. Federal, state, and local governments are the largest employers of professionals in the United States. This development has affected accountability and responsibility. Professionals often report to "lay" superiors and the profession's ability to render judgment about the nature of the individual's practice, or to discipline its members, has been reduced. Professional men and women want to be regarded as part of an independent self-regulating profession *but at the same time* they want the security of a salary and benefits provided by an organization. However, there is inconsistency in wanting it both ways; the independence and self-regulation fundamental to a profession is relinquished by the quest for institutional security. The institutionalization of the professions is one of the most significant contemporary developments in American society because of the long-term impact it has, not only on the nature of the professions, but also on the nation's social policy.

The four factors I have enumerated are all contemporary developments in the professions which have affected the traditional definition of a profession. A crisis of identity exists among individual practitioners and within the professions as a whole. Public scrutiny, demands for regulation, problems with the deployment of professionals, and troubles resulting from an imbalance between supply and demand require new thinking about what it is to be a physician, attorney, or minister. Professional education, in particular, suffers from the lack of a clear idea about the nature of its products.[10] The job of a professional school is not only to impart knowledge, but also to socialize. But socialization presupposes clarity about the group into which one is socialized.[11] If a profession is confused about its identity, its professional schools will accordingly be less effective.

The four reasons I have cited in this section on contemporary developments point to a gap between the traditional definition of what it means to be a professional and the realities of modern society. It may be that part of the answer to the crisis in the professions can be found in a careful consideration of the factors that originally identified a profession. In doing so, I think it can be demonstrated that the problem of ethics is fundamental. The real crisis in the professions has to do with the nature of practice, the way that practice is perceived by the lay public, and the social policy questions that arise accordingly.

In this chapter, I have explored the traditional definition of a profession and noted some of the problems with the definition in our contemporary society. The problems with the traditional definition are in its application because there are significant ethical demands of the professional idea. In fact, these demands derive from Christian principles and are the foundations on which the professions are built. Any consideration of ethics and the professions should start at the beginning. The Christian ethical guidelines which are inherent in the meaning of what it is to be a professional are not often articulated, let alone pondered. It should be recognized, however, that the loss of the professional heritage may be one reason for the crisis in professional ethics.

Despite the fact that not all professionals fit easily within the definition I have given, I suggest that "professional" is a positive adjective, and that professional competence is vital to society. Without men and women who have knowledge, and who have the skill to apply that knowledge in a way that represents and cares for the enduring values of the culture, society is in a precarious position. A sense of the richness and vitality of the notion of the true professional needs to be rekindled in contemporary American society.

2

THE CONTEMPORARY CRISIS
IN THE PROFESSIONS

A gap is between the traditional definition of a profession and the way in which the professions function in the late twentieth century. This gap contributes to the problems in the professions because neither professionals nor the lay public are equipped to think in new ways about the role of the professions. Old images do not fit new realities. The reasons for the gap between traditional theory and present reality are complex, but it is necessary to understand these factors if we are to attempt to move toward a Christian approach to professional practice.

Secularization and Pluralism:
The Absence of Shared Values

Contemporary American society, and indeed all of Western culture is dominantly secular, if by secular we mean that official and public conceptions of common life are not fundamentally informed by a theological vision. Multiple competing views of reality, in a society in which no one view can command the ultimate loyalty of a majority, result in a pluralism of meanings and values. This pluralism is problematic for common life because of its essential tendency toward relativism. That is, multiple points of view about values and meanings are, at least officially, accorded equal value. For the professions this absence of shared values is a serious problem.

In the twentieth century, bureaucracy, rational economic systems, rapid transportation, mass communication, and high-level technology have produced, in vast numbers of men and women, little interest or inclination to seek anything other than material reality. Religious affirmations are not meaningful to people who believe that "what *is* is *now*, and there *is* no *more.*" Secularization is the process by which men and women, and institutions of society, give up religious descriptions of reality. In the last chapter, I observed that perhaps the greatest difficulty modern men and women have in understanding medieval people has to do with the fact that the Middle Ages were not secular. The Christian view of the world was the prevailing orthodoxy and all aspects of personal and social life were accordingly defined. Secularization gradually ended the monopoly of the Christian picture of reality in Western civilization.

Historians of religion suggest that Judaism and Western Christianity, above all Protestantism, carried within themselves the seeds of secularism. These religions of monotheism, by removing from the world spirits, demons, and lesser gods, opened the gates for the long trek to the time when, in the nineteenth century, some thinkers would even posit the absence, or death, of God. Men and women came to think of themselves as self-sufficient and capable of self-development. Protestantism's insistence on perpetual examination of accepted doctrines resulted in a permanent fragmentation of the church in the West. Challenges to the teaching authority of the church encouraged a spirit of criticism which could not be confined to the church and gave rise to skepticism. The critical spirit invaded all domains and its impact was not limited to the intellectual elite.

We live in a time when no one description of ultimate reality prevails. The Christian view of the world competes not only with other religious ideas of reality, but also with ideas that are hostile to religion. Our world is pluralist, and because it is pluralist, secular values become the only common denominator by which motives for action can be publicly justified. Western political leaders, for instance, cannot argue the rightness of their acts simply by appeals to revealed religion. Secular culture has segmented life into private and public spheres. Religion is regarded as appropriate in the private sphere. Thus one's religious beliefs are personal and private and are not permitted intrusion into common life.

Currently sociologists and historians of religion are discussing whether or not secularization is inevitable and irreversible. Some observers point to elements in Western culture that suggest religious revival. Perhaps the most notable development is the growth of evangelical religion and conservative churches in the United States. The importance of this growth for our discussion of secularization is that some conservative leaders suggest that their Christian moral values should be enforced by law, since, they claim, these values are held by a majority of Americans.

In the past, conservative Christianity coexisted with a secular social order because it compartmentalized life. Christian fellowship, worship, and belief occupied only a portion of one's total life. The demands of the Christian life were understood as personal and private, essentially between the individual Christian and God, and they did not compete with one's work, family, or other aspects of life. The success of the conservative evangelical movement may be dependent on its willingness not to make radical claims which challenge the life-style of the middle-class American of the late twentieth century.

A notable movement of persons committed to challenge secularism and to champion traditional moral values is the "Moral Majority." Claiming to be open to anyone, the movement is primarily made up of conservative Christians. The "Moral Majority" proposes to have social impact and to take seriously government power to shape society. What is sought is the recovery of official shared values on which moral judgments can be made. Most importantly, the official shared values are to be those given by God, as interpreted by conservative Christians. That the "Moral Majority" is influential is unquestionable; whether it will be able to overcome the predominant pluralism in American society is yet to be seen.

Another recent challenge to modernism and secular culture on behalf of a religion is that attempted in the 1979 revolution in Iran led by Ayatullah Ruhollah Khomeini. The idea was to eradicate the division between religion and the rest of life and to establish a theocratic Islamic republic. Khomeini's revolution can be understood as a cultural revolution against the movement toward a secular state on the part of the deposed Shah. I mention this effort because it is an attack on secular values by a major religious leader who believes that the well-being of his religion depends on rejecting the secularism of the West.

One need not approve of Khomeini or his revolution to notice that it is a significant event in the story of religion in the modern world. Islam, like Christianty, is in crisis over the relationship between religion, culture, and values. The gradual secularization of culture that the West has experienced for the past two hundred years is now confronting the Arab countries that are encountering the

West with money to invest in technology, travel, and modernization. It remains to be seen whether efforts such as that of Khomeini can prevent the secularization of Islamic nations. The likelihood, it seems to me, is not great. The brutal tactics the Ayatullah has employed suggest that there are serious problems with attempts to recover lost reality.

The modern alternative to society in which there is one prevailing world view is society in which plural world views exist together. Pluralism tolerates and encourages a variety of world views. No one set of organizing ideas, or symbols, can command the loyalty of a nation of modern men and women. The implications for religion are profound. Before the twenties, Americans thought of their nation as a Protestant empire.[1] Although serious differences of opinion surfaced and social policy issues were a source of perpetual conflict, a person could engage his or her opponents in a common discourse with confidence that meanings would be shared and understood. We cannot now assume common discourse or meanings even among Christians.[2]

Many groups claim to have religious truth and each of them claims as well to know the way life should be lived. How can an individual, or a society, know which is ultimately true? How is one to judge among competing views of reality and their various ethical recommendations? The inability to answer these questions in a way that is convincing to a majority of Americans has contributed to a crisis in morality.

Relativism proposes that competing world views and their ethical teachings are equal in value, if they are considered in a theoretical and impartial manner. Individuals may choose particular views of reality, but none is so convincing as to compel universal loyalty. Secularization, pluralism, and relativism are thus inseparable and together present a serious problem for ethics. The ability to make judgments about moral actions depends upon shared values which can serve as guidelines for argument. Unless judgments can be made about moral decisions, they are not *moral* decisions, but simply decisions of individual idiosyncrasy. Ethical reflection requires clearly stated assumptions to which one can appeal when reasons for action are examined.

We have seen that the traditional definition of a profession grew out of a culture in which shared values were grounded in the Christian view of reality. Even in American society, until the twentieth century, professional authority was based on the assumption that practitioners and the lay public had *a history of shared values* that in turn was based on the Judeo-Christian tradition. These values served the professions and, in turn, were served by the professions. A moral tradition can no longer be assumed, in large part because the religious world view from which it derives has been relativized by secularization and pluralism. The absence of a common moral tradition which provides a starting point for ethical analysis has contributed to the crisis of ethics in the professions.

Challenges to Professional Authority

Professional authority in Western society has been dependent on the claim, fundamental to the traditional definition, that a professional is competent and dedicated. Competence derived from years of education and practical training and concerned cognitive and manual skills. Dedication had to do with the essential ethical component of a profession and provided one who sought the services of a professional with reasonable assurance that his or her best interests would be served. Dedication to the professional ideal was meaningful because it was based on the shared values of the society. Professionals were respected because they were the best educated men in the community and the lay community was dependent upon them to fulfill needs that could be met in no other manner.

In contemporary America, both the competence and dedication of the professional class is being challenged by the lay public. The general level of education has risen to the point that lay men and women can understand matters that once they left to professionals. Continuing examinations of professional competence and public exposure to criticism of the professions from within their own ranks have resulted in a growing skepticism of professional dominance. The resort to legal action in cases charging physicians with malpractice is an example of a fundamental challenge to professional competence. Malpractice suits have escalated dramatically in the past two decades. The reasons are manifold and have to do with the desire of attorneys to accept the cases and the willingness of members of the medical profession to criticize colleagues; but the underlying reason is that the American public is not willing to accept unquestioningly the claims of competence on the part of the physicians.

The challenge to professional competence has contributed to the undermining of professional authority, but perhaps even more damaging has been the attack on professional dedication. Professionals historically have been regarded as dedicated persons who could be trusted to care for the best interests of those who were served. Popular conceptions of professional men and women no longer fit the ideal. If there is uncertainty about professional

competence, there is even greater skepticism about the
dedication of professionals. The absence of shared values
has brought about a lack of confidence that the professional
practitioner can be trusted. Reports abound of unnecessary
surgery, unreliable dental practice, questionable legal
advice, and poor-quality teaching. The phrase "caveat
emptor," let the buyer beware, was historically limited to
the business community. Merchantile interests were
understood to be different from the interests of the
professional class. The *buyer* needed to beware of the
claims of the seller because the public was not convinced of
the ethical dedication of the merchant. The professional
was set apart because he represented a tradition of service.
Now this tradition of service often appears overridden by
self-service, and confidence in the professions has been
eroded. Professional men and women have been "demyth-
ologized." By this I mean that the doctor, lawyer, minister,
teacher, dentist, and professor are not as apt to be
surrounded with an aura of respect and admiration as they
once were. Their competence and dedication are no longer
accepted uncritically and their authority accordingly has
been undermined.

The Call for Regulation

We have seen how the absence of shared values and
changed conditions in contemporary America have
undermined confidence in professional competence and
dedication. Professional authority is so thoroughly challenged that one often hears calls for external regulation of
the professions. We explored the traditional definition of a
profession and learned that the idea of autonomy is
fundamental. Autonomy means that the profession is free

to set its own standards for education and competence and to establish its own methods of internal discipline. The lack of trust with which the public views the professions has resulted in demands that some guarantees be offered that professional service be trustworthy.

In one sense, the professions are already regulated. Physicians must meet standards of licensing and be accredited for practice. Attorneys must be admitted to the bar and meet state requirements which are established by legislatures and administered by state agencies. But recent calls for regulation of the professions are more far-reaching. The challenge to professional competence and dedication results in demands for increased control of the professions by the government. Unless professional men and women understand the *reasons* for the calls for regulation, they will not be able responsibly to address themselves to the problem. The official professional societies that oppose change are perceived as bastions of selfishness dedicated to the preservation of privilege and wealth.

Terence C. Halliday, a researcher for the American Bar Foundation thinks it is only a matter of time until the federal government will exert stronger regulatory control over the practice of law in the United States. "The legal profession," he says, "is at a moral crossroads. If it doesn't change its attitude and make some radical changes in its delivery of services to the poor, a government-sponsored legal insurance program similar to Medicaid will be initiated." Distrust of attorneys has resulted in widespread calls for regulation to protect the public.

The purpose of this chapter is to explore the factors that have contributed to the contemporary crisis in the professions. We have seen that Americans now lack a shared moral tradition. The absence of a certainty about common values has contributed to a profound skepticism about professional competence and dedication. This, in turn, has brought forth demands for external control to protect the public. Calls for regulation of the professions stem from the same positive motives as calls to regulate all manner of people and things in American society; but for the professions, demands for external regulation are particularly problematic because of the strong, traditional idea that self-regulation is fundamental.

Professional Education: Access and Ethical Formation

Professional schools serve two major functions for any profession. In the first place, they are the gateway to practice because they award necessary credentials. In the second place, they are the centers of research and development for the profession. No profession is without a training program. In the case of law, medicine, and theology, training is frequently within a university. All professions undergo perpetual renewal as intellectual, technological, and social changes occur. While there is a constant tension between theory and practice, those who hold posts in the front-rank schools of a profession are looked to for leadership in research and continuing education. Our rapidly changing society has made it necessary for professional associations to mandate regular education beyond the period of training-in-course. This work with established practitioners has become a major function of the professional schools.

The present status of the American professional school is a twentieth-century development. As we saw in the first chapter, the learned professions were an integral part of the medieval university; but the professions became increasingly practical, and the argument for advanced university training was difficult to sustain. In early America, moreover, there were no universities. The institutions of higher learning were designed to prepare men for the ministry and, while they were called liberal arts colleges, their curriculum demonstrates that they functioned as seminaries. *New England's First Fruits* (1643) bears witness to this fact when it explains the reason for the founding of Harvard College in 1636:

> After God had carried us safe to New England and we had builded our houses, provided necessaries for our livelihood, reared covenient places for God's worship, and settled the civil government; one of the next things we longed for and looked after was to advance learning and perpetuate it to posterity, dreading to leave an illiterate ministry to the churches when our present ministers shall lie in the dust.[3]

As time went on, and more students who did not intend to be clergymen entered college, the colleges became less professionally oriented. Baccalaureate education came to be understood as preparation for a number of occupations which served the commonwealth, and specific training in divinity became a function of graduate work.

Professional schools began to take root in the late eighteenth century, though nineteenth-century training for the professions was considerably different from what we know now. The professions lacked real organization, and standards of access were nonexistent. There was no consensus on a body of knowledge essential to the practice of a profession. The established colleges were unsure about how to add professional departments, and practitioners were skeptical of too much education. Access to the professions normally was through apprenticeship. If a young man desired to be a physician, he worked with a doctor until he learned the practice of medicine. The level of education for medicine was not great, and its practice was haphazard until early in our own time. Medicine was more art than science. A common observation is that, in the late nineteenth century, the chances were less than 50 percent that an average patient seeing an average physician would benefit from the encounter. Law, too, required little erudition unless one aspired to juridical theory. The young lawyer characteristically read for the bar under the guidance of a practitioner. Theology remained a profession requiring learning, though even the clergy devised ways of lessening the theoretical study required of some parish ministers so that a two-track system developed in which theological scholars attained a degree while ministers who were destined to more practical tasks often prepared for ordination through apprenticeship. Many clergy lacked even rudimentary education. The apprentice system served both the practitioners and the students, but the quality of professional practice was uneven and left much room for improvement.

Educators and leaders in the profession believed that progress would come through professional associations and schools. The University of Pennsylvania began a rudimentary medical college in 1765. King's College, later Columbia University, followed in 1767. Yale's "Medical Institution" was established in 1810. The early nineteenth century witnessed the founding of numerous theological seminaries; and one could write the history of theology in America with reference to the reasons for which seminaries were begun. Yale Divinity School became a separate branch of Yale College in 1822, and a law school was initiated in 1824. Many colleges developed professional departments in the course of the nineteenth century, though the standards at these schools were not high and admission was virtually open to all comers.

Perhaps the most decided single advance in professional education in America came in 1876 with the founding of The Johns Hopkins University in Baltimore. This institution was modeled after the Germany university, and was designed primarily to serve graduate students. Most of the other American institutions were adaptations, designed for undergraduates, of English collegiate education. The Johns Hopkins Medical School, founded 1893, brought about a revolution in graduate professional education by introducing stringent standards and scientific excellence. Developments at Johns Hopkins led the way for the famous Abraham Flexner Report of 1910. The Flexner Report was a careful study of medical education in America. Its findings instigated considerable reform. A number of medical schools, which were little more than diploma mills, closed, and others sought to raise standards by adopting the Johns Hopkins model. Distinguished American medical schools are thus products of the early years of the twentieth century, and those which were founded early had no advantage over those founded later.

Medicine is a good example of the process of professionalization. Once the professional schools became more exacting and consolidated the leadership of the profession, associations were developed to raise professional standards. It is well to remember that professional associations were begun to guarantee the public better service through rigorous demands for high-quality education and practice. Only later would these associations appear primarily interested in the protection of professional privilege. Associations of doctors urged legislatures to enact laws governing the licensing of physicians. This was opposed by some who argued that the effort was elitist and designed to help the medical schools; but the fact is that the work of these pioneering physicians meant that the quality of practice was significantly advanced and public safety considerably enhanced.

Critics of the medical schools, often doctors without rigorous training, were right to think that improved standards in the profession would raise the status and importance of professional schools. Later when a degree from a professional school was required for admission to a profession, the power of the schools became great. The professional school admissions committee may be the most difficult hurdle for the person who wishes to enter a profession. Despite their problems, the professions remain popular and the demand for admission to the nation's finest professional schools continues to exceed the number of available places. A letter of admission from a prestigious school is popularly viewed as a ticket to success and wealth. It is difficult to prognosticate about occupations, but most evidence suggests that the demand for professional education will continue to be strong. The number of young men and women entering schools of law, medicine, or divinity may, in fact, exceed reasonable estimates of the need for professionals in the future.

Currently over 360,000 physicians are practicing in the United States. Medical schools have prevented the supply of doctors to exceed demand and therefore physicians whose average income in 1980 was $80,800 remain America's best-paid professionals.[4] Recently medical schools reported a slight decline in applications, but this may reflect recognition on the part of some prospective students that an application is a waste of time. Estimates of the need for physicians for the future vary. The Bureau of Labor Statistics' *Occupational Outlook Handbook* suggests that there could be a 37.8 percent increase in jobs for physicians from 1976 to 1985. That statistic is misleading, however, because it does not take into account America's severe maldistribution of medical personnel. Some of the predicted jobs are in, what some consider to be, undesirable locations.

The prospects for future attorneys is less bright. Over 521,000 lawyers are in America, and in the next decade job prospects for qualified law graduates are not altogether good. Obviously, many young lawyers will get fine jobs, but the possibilities are diminishing. The legal profession will experience about 25 percent growth between 1976 and 1985, but law schools will turn out many more graduates than there are jobs.[5] As in the field of medicine, job opportunities that do exist will often be in small towns and rural communities. Perhaps the restricted opportunities in major urban centers will result in a better distribution of professional people.

The future for the clergy is also difficult to predict. Women now account for over 40 percent of the theological students, but the total number of students has remained virtually the same. This means that the number of men entering the ministry has declined in the past decade. While some churches, such as the Protestant Episcopal Church, have far too many clergy for the positions available, others, such as The United Methodist Church, continue to have many opportunities. The Roman Catholic Church is experiencing a shortage of clergy. The rule of celibacy imposes an additional qualification, however, which goes beyond demands made of other professionals.[6]

In the past decade the number of women entering all the professional schools has increased sharply. Women make up half of the student bodies of a number of law schools. In medicine, business, and graduate schools of arts and sciences, women usually are one-fourth to one-third of the entering class. It is yet too early to make definitive statements about the impact of large numbers of women on the professions. Career patterns for women may be different, especially if some choose to combine marriage and family with professional careers. Nevertheless, the influx of women into the professional schools has altered the procedure governing admission, the character and attitude of the faculties, and, sometimes, the nature of the curricula.

We have seen that the professional schools are in a position of strength and influence because they are the gateway to practice. For this reason, the admission process has become the center of considerable controversy. The crisis of access to the professions is being borne by the schools. Many more people are seeking entry into professional education than the professional schools can accommodate. Moreover, efforts to increase the number of blacks, hispanics, and other minorities in the professions have brought heavy pressures on admissions committees to guarantee that a certain number of places in each class go to minority persons. Such a social policy decision may have considerable merit for the long-range good of the nation, but who should make such a decision? Should the admissions procedures of the nation's professional schools be invested with such far-reaching authority? To the white student denied access because a certain number of places are reserved for minority candidates, the process appears unjust. Denial of admission alters life plans and aspirations. The famous case in which Allan Bakke sued the regents of the University of California because he was denied access to medical school, even though his "objective" qualifications were better than minority candidates who were admitted, epitomizes the problem. Recently age has surfaced as another issue. Some professional schools have tended to reject applicants on the basis of their age, but older men and women are challenging the legitimacy of allowing age to be a factor in the admission decision.

As controllers of access to important institutions of American society, the professional schools are agents of a kind of social engineering. The dilemma of admissions, which has resulted in numerous suits, has been aggravated by efforts to remove personal factors from the process. Because of the enormous number of applications, the schools have devised means of admitting on the basis of relatively "objective" criteria such as rank in class, grades, and the famous tests of the Educational Testing Service. Such criteria are convenient and usable, but, as educators know, there is no indication that persons who excel on tests will make good practitioners. The crisis of access is heightened by the idea that "objective" criteria are used to make decisions. Perhaps personal and social policy considerations have a legitimate role to play in the admissions process. Admittedly, as the courts have demonstrated, such considerations involve complex delib-eration, but the good of both the professions and the nation may best be served by a frank recognition that other factors than "objective" criteria can and should enter into admissions decisions. The compelling need for more highly trained black physicians is one example; so is the need for some physicians who see practice as service and who desire to practice general medicine in non-urban settings. The present system of admission to professional schools too often does not encourage the kind of diversity that could enrich the professions. A careful examination of the assumptions that govern admissions could have important implications for the nature of professional practice in America.

In addition to the problem of access, professional education is currently faced with challenges concerning the ethical formation of prospective practitioners. The most pressing issue facing the professions today is the matter of *style*. I defined style as having to do with the way both colleagues and laypeople perceive professional practice. The crisis in professional authority results from a lack of public confidence about the trustworthiness and dedication of practitioners. Does the professional school have a responsibility to teach ethics? Is the formation of character a proper concern of those who train lawyers, physicians, ministers, engineers, or teachers? Style, which determines the moral as well as the technical shape of practice, is determined by the character of the professional life. Education in America has always emphasized practicality, but perhaps now more than ever, colleges and universities are being perceived as places where one prepares for making a living rather than living a life. New efforts to confront the moral dimension reflect the desire of growing numbers of Americans to ponder matters that deal with the quality of life as well as the material quantity of life. Those involved in professional education are being called on to think in new ways about the needs and possibilities of teaching ethics as a part of training-in-course.

A special task force of the American Bar Association,

chaired by Dean Roger C. Cramton of Cornell University Law School, and composed of lawyers, judges, and law deans, recently called on law schools to redesign their curricula to provide prospective attorneys with integrated learning experiences combining regular course work with outside learning. The professional school experience would thus be broadened and would equip students to deal more competently with rapidly changing societal conditions. Moreover, the commission emphasized the need for "fostering constructive work habits, attitudes and values." The report calls for a change in the attitude of law faculties which have largely ignored ethics, except with reference to matters of propriety or etiquette. Indeed, by selecting the word "values," the commission implies concern for the moral formation of future attorneys.

Some medical schools have moved toward the inclusion of courses in philosophical and biomedical ethics, although such work is not a mandatory part of the curriculum. Nevertheless, the pressing issues of medical ethics are compelling educators to think about effective ways of incorporating ethical training in medical education and a number of schools have already named to their faculties trained ethicists who hold the Ph.D. degree in religion or philosophy.

Derek Bok, the president of Harvard University, recently selected the Harvard Business School as the focus of his *Annual Report*. The report is far-ranging, but among the emphases is the teaching of ethics. Bok has long been an advocate of incorporating training for ethical analysis within undergraduate and professional education.[7] Bok argues that ethics should be an important ingredient of the Business School's course of study:

The thing is to build into the faculty people who have a training both in moral philosophy and a knowledge of business. If the person's base is only in philosophy, you have been putting people to sleep and if his base is only in business, he will be saying things that are ethically naive. The only way to get at this is to hire some Ph.D.'s in moral philosophy and give them training in the business school. This way the students from these people's courses will raise ethical issues with professors in other courses and those professors will have fellow faculty members to whom they can turn for advice.

The value of, and need for, the kind of training Bok writes about is not lost on faculty and students. The Business School has been seeking ways of incorporating the teaching of ethics in the curriculum. For a number of years, in response to an annual survey, nearly 60 percent of the first-year business students requested more discussion of ethical issues in the classroom.[8]

Consideration of ethical formation in the professional schools requires making a careful distinction between the *process of ethical reasoning* and the *development of moral values*. The process of ethical reasoning surely can be taught; this is what Derek Bok advocates. One effective way is through the use of a case method in which a dilemma is posed and the ethical issues are sorted and evaluated. Students can be taught a process of analysis which allows one to distinguish reasonable arguments cogently set forth from emotive, idiosyncratic, personal opinion. The moral issues that arise in various ways and places within professional schools involve such matters as the impact of the profession as a whole on the society, relationships between the practitioner and the individual client as a person, relationships among colleagues in one's own profession and among colleagues from other professions, and issues of personal versus institutional responsibility for professionals who work within large organizations. The teaching of ethics is not an endeavor to teach, or inculcate, particular moral values.

It is often the case, however, that ethical reflection moves one beyond the description of moral issues toward normative, prescriptive value judgments. If it does not do so, it is simply philosophical investigation.[9] Such a move involves the introduction of foundational moral traditions.

I mean by this that, if one ever is to go beyond the *process of ethical reasoning* to *moral content* that can allow *normative judgment*, one inevitably must consider systems of belief and value. Traditionally, religious communities have fulfilled this role. In the West, Judeo-Christian teachings have given content to ethical judgments. Secularism and pluralism now complicate the moral picture. The professional schools, in effect, must seek to train students in *ethical analysis* even while they avoid sanctioning a particular set of *moral values*. One could argue that official pluralism, which now predominates in American thought, is a strong affirmation of relativism and is thus not itself value-free at all. Nevertheless, the teaching of ethical analysis *can* be done apart from prescriptive judgment and such training can greatly enhance the competence of a professional person in practice. Continuing professional education holds much promise as an occasion when seasoned professionals together can do ethical analysis of cases and learn from experienced ethicists and from one another.

Training in the moral traditions of specific communities, such as Christianity, which undergird ethics with patterns of belief needs to be done among professional colleagues who share commitments. As I indicated in the introduction, that is one reason for this book. How might a Christian physician or lawyer, for instance, who is skilled in the tools of ethical reasoning, approach a specific moral dilemma growing out of professional practice? Some specific reflection about the professions in America and professional ethics within the Christian community is needed.

PART
TWO

CHRISTIAN THEOLOGY
AND
PROFESSIONAL
RESPONSIBILITY

3

EDUCATING FOR THE MORAL LIFE

The contemporary crisis in the professions results from challenges to the traditional idea of a profession and new social and intellectual realities. I have suggested that the heart of the problem has to do with conflicting values and moral ambiguity. To advance our consideration of ethics and the professions, it will be helpful to identify some of the issues that present themselves in any effort to deal with morality and ethics.

The Inevitability of Moral Education

A "moral situation" is an occasion that calls forth ethical analysis. Moral situations are not unusual; they are a part of daily experience. Three examples will be useful.

Not long ago, I read an account in the newspaper of two young men who were on their way home from work at a local shopping center. As they drove along a four-lane street toward the center of the city, they suddenly saw a car ahead of them go out of control and slam into a telephone pole. The two young men pulled their car to the side of the road and rescued a man and woman from the wrecked car just as the car was about to burst into flames. Unable to extricate themselves from the wreckage without the help of the young men, the couple would have burned to death. After the incident, a newspaper reporter felt bound to ask the question, "Why did you stop?"

It was a legitimate question. The hour was late on a Saturday night, the young men were tired and anxious to get home. So many stories are told today of "good Samaritans" whose efforts to help turn to nightmares that many people are hesitant to come to the aid of persons in trouble. Nevertheless, the young men stopped, and in response to the reporter's question, one of them answered, "I *stopped because my father would have stopped.*" Reflecting on his action, the reason he gave for a particular moral decision had to do with observation and imitation of his father.

The second example of a moral situation comes from a time when I was invited to speak at a liberal arts college noted for its preprofessional training. Before I spoke, I chatted with the dean in his office. He expressed the hope that I would say something about honesty in higher education. He explained that the college was having acute problems with cheating in premedical courses. One student was caught destroying a laboratory experiment of a fellow student. Confronted by the judicial board, which inquired as to why he had cheated, the student replied, *"Everybody is doing it."*

The third example is a moral situation involving public policy. I participated in a colloquium in a small town in which we discussed a number of issues relating the humanities to social policy. Perhaps because I was the only theologian among the group of professors who comprised the panel, one woman addressed a question to me about sex education in the public schools. That was not the topic of the colloquium, but we soon learned it was the topic of the moment. I did not immediately offer my own observations on the question, but sought to use the occasion as an example of a moral dilemma. I asked the questioner her own ideas and she replied only that she was unalterably opposed to sex education in the schools. She said, *"Such information implicitly condones premarital sex."*

How might one evaluate, "My father would have done it," or "Everybody is doing it"? What moral reasons and arguments are hidden behind, "Such information implicitly condones premarital sex"?

Each of these moral situations offers an opportunity to analyze the reasons for which an individual takes a position or does an act. The situations demonstrate that one does not have to be a trained ethicist to be called on to give reasons for moral action or position. Moreover, in each of the situations one can see a distinction between moral action and ethical reflection.

What causes us to act in one way or another? What is the process by which we learn to act in certain ways? Where do we get our moral ideas? What causes us to think in particular ways about moral action? How do we learn to express ourselves about moral acts and to give reasons for what we do? What is the relationship, if any, between what we think about moral action and what we do when we act?

These questions lead to consideration of moral education and development. There are two major areas of concern, the first is pedagogical, the second is institutional.[1] The first has to do with whether and in what way morality can be taught. The second has to do with which persons and which institutions should be charged with moral education.

It is not clear whether morality can be taught, if we mean by that the training of young people into patterns of voluntary behavior which are "good," "right," or "desirable." No evidence indicates that moral instruction guarantees moral persons. Many persons' home life, religious training, and schooling appear exemplary, but their values and actions are contrary to those taught.

Despite the problems, inconsistencies, and uncertainties about moral education, attention to virtues, moral discernment, and more explicitly, the "good," as opposed to "bad," has always been accorded significance and value by human societies. Perhaps this is so because societies have been unwilling to leave moral education to chance. Human beings seem to want to articulate values which often go unspoken. Moreover, particular communities, such as religious traditions, have specific values they want to impart to their children. Although it is unclear to what extent morality can be taught, generations have tried rather than take the risk of not doing so.

Moral education is inevitable in the sense that the multiple institutions of society communicate, both explicitly and implicitly, values which have implication for action. These institutions include the family, religious communities, schools, mass media, and all manner of voluntary associations. Persons are exposed to these multiple institutions and the relationship among them is not simple. On occasion one hears it said that failure in family life has made the school the centerpiece of moral education, or that the government is misusing the public schools by making them vehicles of value-laden social change.

Recently I was lecturing to a group when a man raised his hand and said, "Don't you think that the best moral learning is that which comes in the home?" That morning I had read a particularly heartrending account of pathological child abuse in a rural town in Michigan. I explained to the questioner that I knew what he meant, but that, in fact, such a statement was too general to be helpful. It depends, of course, on the nature of the home, and on what values one brings to an evaluation of the home. My questioner was trying to say that the Christian home is the best place for moral education to take place. But notice the hidden values his statement implies. I would take them to include at least these:

1. A Christian home is founded on a permanent, monogamous marriage between a Christian man and woman

2. A Christian home is open to the inclusion of children

3. A Christian home includes training of its children in the meaning and practice of Christian faith

4. A Christian home is related to the ongoing life of a local congregation in which further moral instruction takes place

One might add other descriptive characteristics, but my point is demonstrated. The original statement included a host of *unexpressed value assumptions*. Such assumptions are common; attention to casual conversation reveals how pervasive they are. Value assumptions are present in all formal and informal educational experiences. There is, accordingly, no value-free education; all education is moral education. The decision to teach one thing rather than another involves a question of values. It is important to understand the value-laden character of all educational experience so that wrong assumptions about what is taking place are avoided. Often there is a difference in what is being taught by the several institutions to which young people are exposed. Modern institutions are not univocal in regard to values.

American society traditionally has liked to assume that the values held and communicated by family, church, public school, the press, and voluntary associations, such as

Scout programs, are the same. American social and intellectual history demonstrates that, in fact, during the nineteenth and early twentieth centuries there was some truth to this. Society was more homogeneous and the ideal was to incorporate newcomers into an American democratic "faith," the rudiments of which informed all institutions of the society.[2] The assumptions of this American tradition were radically challenged in the decades after World War II, and particularly in the late 1960s. One cannot now assume shared values in American society. The society is dominantly secular; and pluralism and relativism have affected virtually all areas of American common life. The moral teachings of the various institutions of society can be confusing, contradictory, and uncertain.

Recognition of the inevitability of moral education has resulted in a remarkable development among professional educators at all levels, from preschool to graduate, professional education, and continuing education. Concern for the nature of values communicated, or the "hidden curriculum," has produced a series of interesting proposals.[3] One of the most famous of these is the *"value clarification"* approach of Sidney Simon in which children are taught, through a variety of games, simulations, and exercises to examine their feelings, values, and behavior patterns.[4] Perhaps the other most well-known proposal for moral education is the work of Lawrence Kohlberg in *moral development*. This approach is based on the idea that people move through moral stages of life. The development is sequential. Kohlberg believes that it is possible for persons to grow toward the more advanced stages through exercises of structured, rational discussion requiring research, analysis, and reasoned argument.[5]

Other approaches to values education are less well-known, but are influential because they include curriculum proposals for school use. The wide range of moral education models is evidence of growing interest in the field and concern about values education in the society.[6] The "hidden curriculum" is being exposed. The moral education movement is itself value-laden, of course. Most obviously, all approaches to moral education are built on the judgment that examined values are preferable to unexamined values. But moral education encourages students to examine the process of moral education itself. The implications for education, in general, and professional education, in particular, can result in significant renewal of curricula.

Professionals are often uninformed and inarticulate in regard to the moral language of their work. In their development as persons and as professionals, they acquired values which inform their practice. The values are often unarticulated and usually not related systematically to the ethical issues of their work. Accordingly, they are unable to think clearly about the important moral issues with which they deal daily. Their responses to ethical query are not unlike the spontaneous and unexamined replies in the three examples of moral situations with which I began this chapter. To be a professional is to deal with matters of moral import; to do so well requires sophistication in ethical analysis.

The Necessity of Ethical Analysis

Ethical analysis is reflection on moral action. It is different from living a moral life. We have seen that education for moral living is complex and there is no certainty that it produces moral response. Ethical analysis, however, is a skill which can be taught.

Men and women who intend to be professionals need to learn the language and process of ethical analysis. The preprofessional school might include the development of ethical reflection in relation to specific case studies drawn from practice as well as in relation to major issues facing the profession, as a profession, in the society.

One of the important goals of professional education is to help students become autonomous. By definition, professionals are independent individuals. Often, however, they do not understand this autonomy to have moral implications. The unexamined values of the profession are assimilated and unquestioningly adhered to throughout a lifetime of practice. Professional education is the time for one to develop the capacity to understand one's own values and to relate them meaningfully to one's work. A person develops values before attending professional school and continues to develop them, but a sense of moral autonomy, as a professional, needs to be addressed consciously in the years of professional training.

By moral autonomy I do not mean the radical independence that rejects any conditioning of individual judgment. Moral autonomy involves the willingness to accept insight from other persons and to submit one's own judgment to scrutiny. All persons have normative values. Reflection on specific actions demonstrates how one examines a decision in reference to intention, result, and the foundation values which may have occasioned one act rather than another. A consciousness about values and an intentional application of them characterize a morally mature person. Moral autonomy has reference, then, to the capacity of the self to act authentically and consistently in relation to foundational principles.

Many professional persons in American society are ethically ignorant because they do not know how to think systematically about decisions they must make. I do not mean that professionals are evil or are necessarily making wrong decisions. They are limited in regard to the increasingly difficult situations all professionals face and are unnecessarily burdened by confused minds and troubled consciences.

A pediatric surgeon recently told me about a difficult decision he had to make about surgery on a premature and severely handicapped child of a medical colleague. He indicated that it did not occur to him that a systematic process of analysis could be helpful. He made the decision, of course, but worried about it, almost to distraction, suggesting that he felt his mind was "muddled." Commonly, ethical decision making has been thought of as a matter of individual conscience. Such a truncated view limits the capacity of the professional to deal creatively with a given situation and places unnecessary strain on the relationship between the professional and the persons involved in the case.

Ethical decision making is processional. It is not simply the ability to apply rules to situations, but the ability to make connections and to think critically and carefully about situations. An important component of ethical education is the professional curriculum should help the individual learn to apply one's own values to the process of decision making.

Professional education is giving new attention to the teaching of ethics. A recent study by The Institute of Society, Ethics, and the Life Sciences in Hastings-on-

Hudson, New York, funded mainly by Carnegie Corporation, reports that the decade of the seventies saw the initiation of introductory courses in applied ethics in most professional schools.[7] The report also notes, however, that sometimes these courses are dominated by the etiquette of dealing with colleagues or other professionals and the appropriateness of certain kinds of behavior (such as advertising). Increasingly, professional schools are requiring courses that teach the process of ethical analysis, often using case studies, and sometimes on an interprofessional level. But another dimension to consider is the concern with moral development in relation to professional practice. Such development has to do with the total formation of a new professional.

The term "formation" is as old as the historic conception of profession. The church first used the term to refer to the process of spiritual development that produced character in men and women preparing for religious orders. Formation is the nurturing of persons in ways to help them develop persistent characteristics of moral selfhood—habits, attitudes, and dispositions which become part of their being. In this way, the moral self does not have to reflect extensively about every problem requiring action, but automatically gives the characteristic response developed in the process of formation.[8]

Professional education, especially in the context of the modern, secular university, tends to assume that attention to the moral self is unnecessary and inappropriate—unnecessary because students have already formed morals and inappropriate because morals are an individual matter. The contemporary crisis in the professions mandates new understanding of ethical formation.

In a recent conversation at a law school, I was asked to

ponder the responsibility of the faculty to express its judgment of a student's fitness to be a lawyer apart from his or her academic capacity. In the abstract such a question is difficult to answer; but I replied that it occurred to me that the professional school, by definition, must be concerned with more than the basic academic preparation of students and must attend, in a systematic way, to the whole person who seeks to become a professional. The dangers of such a proposal are obvious. Might prejudice lead people to unfairly judge one who simply does not "fit the system" and who might offer a significant alternative within the profession? It is possible to proliferate objections, but most objections are rooted in the fact that it is difficult to deal with professional candidates as whole persons and easier to attend only to academic performance.

Professional school faculties might usefully address the question of what sort of professional persons they wish to graduate and then examine the curriculum to see where the complex matters of ethics are dealt with and where the total formation of students is considered. The assumption that formation happens naturally through association with faculty, students, and practitioners is only partly adequate. Unless specific attention to formation is given in the heart of the curriculum, it will not be taken seriously by the students or the faculty.

The teaching of ethical analysis can be included in professional education in a number of ways:

1. Education might provide opportunities for students to become aware of the moral implications of the material they are learning. Individual classes could deal with actual cases drawn from practice with the subject at hand featured in a moral dilemma. The school as a whole might designate programmatically for a term a specific problem to serve as

an example for applying a wide range of individual disciplines. Persons from outside could be asked to address the matter, and then faculty and students could talk with each other about the subject in a variety of settings outside of class.

2. Internships, practical experience, and action projects related to the profession need to be more creatively integrated into the total academic program of professional education. The conflict between theory and practice will always be present in professional education. However, the relationship between these modes of education might be enhanced if the question of ethical response became the integrating factor.

3. The professional curriculum should include opportunity for students to study the history and sociology of the profession for which they are preparing. This would include the exploration of the way the profession has developed, the way it has been portrayed in fiction, drama, film, and the press, and the sociological realities which inform it. I have found it beneficial to encourage both students preparing for a profession and current practitioners to read autobiographies of men and women from the profession. A course on the profession itself would be an occasion to explore the ethical questions pertaining to its role in society as well as the role, style, and nature of individual practitioners.

The professional school curriculum is already burdened, but the importance of a course such as the one I describe, carefully developed for the specific profession, would help the student learn about the profession's tradition, current state, and prognosis for the future. It would provide a context for wide ranging, but tightly disciplined, reflection about what it means to become, for instance, a doctor, lawyer, minister, engineer, or professor.

4. Ethical formation for all professional students should include serious and sustained curricular relationship with persons entering other professions. The complex nature of contemporary life militates against natural relationships among professionals. The demands of individual careers too often isolate us from collegiality with our peers and even more so from persons in other professions. Yet it can be argued that the extraordinary nature of so many of the situations demanding professional expertise requires inter-professional expertise. These are usually cases, moreover, in which moral questions are ascendent. One thinks, for instance, of the convergence of legal, medical, and theological issues in the question of the treatment versus non-treatment of the handicapped newborn.

Young professionals need to learn how to work with, understand, appreciate, and accept persons in other professions as colleagues. Interprofessional education is a major opportunity for education in ethical analysis and moral formation.

The Relationship Between Religion and Ethics

Whenever the subject of moral education is considered, the question of the relationship between religion and ethics arises. Perhaps this is so because American culture historically has tended to equate religion and ethics. The reformed Protestant religious tradition which dominated early American foundations placed heavy practical emphasis on the direct relationship between Christian belief and political, social, and personal life. The equation was carried further in the religious revivals called the Great

Awakenings of the eighteenth century, as well as the extraordinary camp meetings and urban evangelistic crusades of the nineteenth century.

In the popular mind of the nineteenth century, to be an American was to be a Protestant, and to be a Protestant was to espouse certain personal moral characteristics. The spirit of the frontier emphasized the "official" outward signs of the sanctified life, including purity in one's sexual life and abstinence from tobacco and beverage alcohol. Even when the church turned its attention to the spheres of politics and society, as in the case of the abolition of slavery, one's overt response to a given moral issue was the test of Christian conviction. This was true for Christian preachers on both sides of an issue, as with slavery. *The point is that religious faith was understood in terms of ethical stance.* It is a mistake, however, to equate religion with ethics. Such an equation results, in the case of Christianity, in a reduction of faith to moral living.

Having Christian faith and living a morally good life are not the same thing.[9] Christian faith is the personal and corporate conviction that leads to confession that God is revealed in Jesus Christ, who is Lord. Christian faith is orientation to, and relationship with, God in Jesus Christ. As a result, everything else is qualified. For one who has faith, the world is seen through eyes that place the exigencies of life in perspective. In the final analysis, God is the sovereign power of all existence; and human life with its artifacts and limited aspirations takes on its true value. That value is dependent upon relationship with God, and there is no other value to compare with it.

Christian faith makes it possible for one to "sit loose" to the triumphs and disappointments, the joys and tragedies of human life. Social, economic, and intellectual dislocation are seen through the eyes of the Christian community. The vision of the church is both backward, toward its foundation in the act of God's Holy Spirit, and forward, toward the consummation of God's love. The blinding transcendent reality of God ever informs the Christian's response to the world.

Throughout our history, Americans have assumed that hard work, right living, and persistence result in economic and social progress. Now, in a time of declining resources, this assumption is not necessarily true either for the individual or for the society. Our social and individual dreams are of material prosperity, of bigger and better things. But because of mushrooming population, indications of energy crisis, inflation, and worldwide economic retrenchment, those dreams may have to be modified, if not fundamentally altered.[10]

This alteration of dreams and expectations is frightening. Fear may be the dominant emotion in our world. It is understandable that this should be so. We stand perpetually at the brink of nuclear annihilation, at worst, or drastically reduced standards of living, at best. Fear is not an emotion that can be overcome with platitudes; it is an emotion that partakes of the most basic matters of value and meaning. Fear is rooted in the sense that men and women cannot control their own destinies. If there is an equation between what one "does" and what one "gets," materially or spiritually, one is in control. If there is no such equation, then one's control is destroyed, and fear may result.

Faith is not built on an equation of "doing" and "getting." Faith is a gift of God. One who has faith is at peace with God because God, alone, is in control. As Paul says, "Since we are justified by faith, we have peace with God through our Lord Jesus Christ" (Rom. 5:1). The love of God helps one achieve a vision that overcomes the paralysis of fear. "Perfect love casts out fear" (I John 4:18). Christian faith includes the power to transcend the ethical and move toward the dimension of the eternal. Such transcendence provides a confident trust that God's grace is the dominant and final reality.

The exigencies of the modern world make it increasingly clear that one whose dependence is on goods and things will be disappointed. The biblical message makes immediate sense in an age of declining resources. To trust in that which can be taken away is to have no abiding object of trust. Most profoundly, to find one's life is to lose it, and to lose it for the sake of Jesus Christ is to find it (Matt. 10:39).

While religion and ethics are not the same thing, the priority of faith means that Christian theology and ethics are fundamentally related. Christian faith is more than moral living, but faith shapes the moral life. This understanding indicates that ethics in general, even theological ethics, is not the same thing as Christian ethics. For the Christian, this distinction is essential, and it has important practical consequences for our consideration of ethics and the professions. This is so because the distinction between ethics and Christian ethics is related to the distinction between general common life and Christian community.

Recognition that Christian community and general common life are not the same thing, and probably can never be, is liberating for the church. Most Christians understand this point, but often a residual desire to talk in terms of a "Christian society" remains. It is an erroneous popular conception that America is a "Christian society." If by "Christian society," one means that a majority of persons indicate that they are Christians in a census, the description is literally accurate. Such identification is not meaningful, however, in Christian terms.

There may be profound truth to the observation that where everyone is a Christian, no one is a Christian. Christian history demonstrates that the most sustained and significant growth of the church occurs in times and places where Christian believers are required to distinguish themselves from the rest of society. The record of the early church is especially dramatic. The astonishing thing about the formative period of the church, during the first four centuries, A.D., is the growth that took place in spite of what appeared historically to be insurmountable odds. Origen, who lived through severe persecution into a time of relative peace, always looked back to the days of trial as a time of triumph:

> The days of real faith were the days when there were many martyrs, the days when we used the take the martyrs' bodies to the cemetery and come straight back and hold our assembly. They were the days when the whole Church was in mourning and the instructions the catechumens received were meant to prepare them to acknowledge their faith right up to the moment of their death, without wavering or faltering in their belief in the living God. Christians saw amazing signs and wonders then, we know. There were few believers then, but they were real ones; they followed the narrow road that leads on to life.[11]

In many modern communities in the West, it is easier for one to affirm Christianity publicly than openly deny it. The easy affirmation of Christianity, however, can result in confusion in the church. The Christian church exists today in a general secular society. Wholesale attacks on the society, or wholesale efforts to change the society are unrealistic. The wisest course of action for the church is attending seriously to the moral actions and responses of the Christian community itself. Christians must seek to influence public policy and engage in political activity; but first of all they need to be clear about what it is they believe and about what it means to act on those beliefs in the complex world in which we live.

This approach is more modest and more realistic than attempts to bring about large-scale moral renewal. It is also, ironically, more difficult because it requires careful reflection on what it means to be a Christian person who must act out one's faith in a society not inclined to understand, or value, action which is so motivated. The dominant attitude on the part of Western culture toward Christianity today is indifference. The church of the late twentieth century has more in common with the early church, which found itself in an indifferent or hostile culture, than with the church of medieval and post-Reformation Western Christendom whose social and intellectual setting permitted it to assume that a nation could be Christian.

Among the implications of this approach to Christian faith and ethics is greater attention on the part of Christian men and women to the relationship between their Christian commitment and the way they live. The Christian professional needs to face the fact that his or her profession, as a whole, cannot, and will not, be reformed in terms of the ethical intentions of Christian faith. This means that professionals in the church have an urgent obligation to explore the particular demands of Christian affirmation on professional style.

This chapter has suggested that it is important for the professional curriculum to include specific training in ethical analysis. Training in ethical analysis can be done in such a way that no particular normative foundation for ethics, such as Christianity, is assumed. This is why ethics can and should be taught in the professional curriculum in which it is neither appropriate, nor possible, to assume homogeneous religious or philosophical foundations and norms.

A danger in the teaching of ethics, however, is that it becomes all form and no content. At some point, questions of *foundations* for values and judgments become important. This concern can be handled in a heterogeneous group through the use of comparative studies and by encouraging individuals to integrate the foundational values and norms that inform their lives with methods of ethical analysis. I am suggesting a precision in the process of teaching ethics which attends to fundamental matters of the systems of belief in which values originate and receive their normative force.

Professional men and women who are Christians need to reflect specifically on the relationship between Christian commitment, the source of normative values, and their work. The reason the learned professions are rooted in religious orders is that they are concerned with both the intimate needs of individual persons and the general needs of the common life. In the language of Christian faith, the professions are forms of ministry. Christian persons are called to the service of God, and the service of others, in total life. Service in total life is living what one believes.

The compartmentalization of modern existence encourages persons to build walls separating the various components of life. Thus one's home, work, leisure, and religious life are often unrelated. Such separation can result in psychological burdens due to the difficulty of maintaining multiple parallel aspects of one life. Christian faith has to do with the integration of multiple aspects of life. Faith's intention for human life is that it be focused upon God in Jesus Christ and find meaning in a singularity of purpose and direction. All aspects of life come together because the Christian self is whole in its relationship to God and to other selves.

The church in the late twentieth century is guilty of permitting compartmentalization to go unchallenged. One of the dominant trends of complex society has been the acquiescence of the church to a peripheral place in the lives of busy persons. The church is one institution among others competing for attention. But for the Christian, the church cannot be understood as simply another institution. The church is *the* community through which God's grace is mediated; it is *the* community of life. The individuals who are the church are dependent, in God, on one another for wholeness. The church reminds us that we are not, finally, *independent* persons, but dependent persons.

For professional persons who are Christians, the importance of this discussion is that moral autonomy is *conditioned* by moral dependence on the norms, judgment, and support of gracious community. To be a Christian and a professional is to expose one's profession to the judgment of the light of faith. For the Christian, educating for the moral life involves training in ethical analysis, but more, it involves training in Christian living. This training points toward God who is both source and norm of all meaning and value; toward God, who relativizes all else; toward God, who conditions all persons. The Christian who is a professional understands that Christian norms and values, apart from the independent inclinations of the individual, or even of the prevailing norms of the profession, must be brought to professional practice.

4

A CHRISTIAN THEOLOGY
OF ACCOUNTABILITY

Norms of Christian Faith

Being a Christian involves the recognition that there are norms external to the self to which the self is accountable. The Christian is accountable, first of all, to God. All Christians would agree that God's authority is absolute. But the intention of God's authority is not given directly to men and women in the world. If it were, there would not be disagreements about what should be believed or what should be done. In fact, considerable disagreements have always existed among Christians because the word of God is mediated to men and women. The process of mediation— the translation of God's intention into concepts and language that can be grasped by human beings—results in a variety of understandings within the church. Dean William Inge, of St. Paul's, London, once remarked, "The Church is absolutely free to make its own rules, without consulting . . . the law of the land. The only authority which it is bound to obey is the law of Christ, and what this is, is by no means clear."[1]

How is one to know the "law of Christ"? How is one to know what to believe and what to do? Through the years, a number of approaches to the question of authority for faith and practice have been advanced. I want to offer an approach to this problem which can be a theological point of initiation for specific problems requiring Christian ethical response.

75

The starting point is the Christian community. The Christian person is a member of the community of faith. One cannot be a Christian apart from the community. On occasion one hears the remark that one can worship God better without the encumbrances of the organized church. The implication of such a remark is that the church is limited and fallible. Of course this is so, but the admission of that fact does not require the further conclusion that the church is dispensable. As Saint Cyprian wrote, "Whoever he may be and whatever he may be, he who is not in the church of Christ is not a Christian."[2] The church is the human community in which and through which God's revelation is mediated, but it is not a human community only. It is divine in that it is established as the agent of God's initiative in the world.

The church expresses its theological self-understanding in its liturgy. The preface to the order used when persons formally become part of the community is an effective theological statement abut the church:

> The Church is of God, and will be preserved to end of time, for the conduct of worship and the due administration of his Word and Sacraments, the maintenance of Christian fellowship and discipline, the edification of believers, and the conversion of the world. All, of every age and station, stand in need of the means of grace which it alone supplies.[3]

The emphasis is upon the church as a divine gift, rather than as a mere human institution. Its preservation depends not on men and women, but on God; and the church, as the instrument of salvation, will endure despite all contrary evidence. Moreover, it is the vehicle of God's grace. All people, no matter who they are, stand in need of grace, thus all stand in need of the ministry of the church. This powerful affirmation assures the priority of the church.

The priority of the church is historical as well as theological. The church was the arena of God's initiating work of Christian revelation in the Holy Spirit after Jesus' crucifixion and resurrection. The community preceded any of the mediating norms. The church was worshiping, preaching, teaching, healing, and serving before the New Testament scriptures, creeds, or other theological writings were initiated.

Christian community is not monolithic, which is to say that there is more than one way of being the church. Because it is at once human and divine, the church manifests itself in a variety of ways in diverse places. In all cases, however, the church is defined by a self-consciousness of Christian identity and intention. To be the church, a community must be intentional about its identity with Christian tradition and its accountability to God and to other Christians. Historically, the church has identified itself as community in which the Word of God is faithfully preached and the Sacraments duly administered.

Some individuals and groups have wanted to go further in specifying the qualifications of "church." These have resulted in distinctive branches of the church. While appreciating the desire to "tighten" the definition and set bounds, I think Christian history demonstrates the wisdom of a certain reticence about becoming narrow. At the same time, there are limits to diversity. A concern for limits prompts the church to attend to norms of faith which provide guidelines for theology and practice. The nature of these norms, and the way in which they work together in the context of Christian community needs now to be given attention.

1. *Bible.* For the earliest Christian community, the Bible was the Jewish scriptures, the thirty-nine books that now comprise what Christians call the Old Testament. The writings that eventually became known as the New Testament, the distinctive scriptures of Christianity, were written after the church was initiated. Determining which writings would be scripture occupied the attention of the church until at least the end of the second century A.D. It is historically accurate, therefore, to speak of the New Testament as a product of Christian community. The term "Christian community," of course, is not merely sociological and historical. As our discussion of the church made clear, *Christian community* is the gracious gift of God. It is the presence of the Holy Spirit that creates Christian community. The scriptures are the written record of God's revelation to, and relation with, the church.

A variety of writings were produced by Christians in the early years of the church's life. Paul's Letters are agreed by scholars to be the earliest of the New Testament writings. These, and some of the later letters written by persons other than Paul, were not written as scripture. The Gospel accounts contained in the New Testament were selected from a number of similar efforts, some of which are extant. These early writers were trying to bring together in a coherent whole the church's proclamation about God in Jesus Christ.

Dating the composition of the New Testament writings is complex. Most biblical scholars, however, are in essential agreement that Paul's letters were written between A.D. 40 and 60, that Mark is approximately A.D. 67, Matthew A.D. 70–80, Luke-Acts, A.D. 80-85, and John A.D. 90-110. Hebrews, Revelation, and the Pastoral Epistles are usually dated A.D. 81-95. The problems of dating are exceedingly complicated, and detailed elaboration of hypotheses require extensive analysis.[4] The above picture nevertheless makes an interesting point: if Jesus' crucifixion and resurrection were approximately A.D. 30, and the gift of the Holy Spirit called the church into being shortly thereafter, the writing of the scriptures came in *response to the Holy Spirit in the life of Christian community.*

Some of the writings that were produced early by the church spoke with exceptional authenticity. These came to be regarded as special gifts from God to the church, and, as such, as authoritative for faith and practice. The church doubtless needed such authoritative writings. It was growing fast, incorporating Gentiles who previously did not know the Jewish scriptures and tradition. In the early church, the concept of God's people was being expanded and conceived in a radically new way to include all men and women in Jesus Christ. The church needed means of organizing in systematic fashion its message, including its understanding of God, of Jesus Christ, and of the Holy Spirit's activity in the creation of the new community.

The word "canon" refers to the authorized books that are regarded as scripture. The Christian canon includes the thirty-nine books of Jewish scriptures, called the Old Testament by the church, and the twenty-seven books of the New Testament. The process by which the church selected from among Christian writings the twenty-seven books which now make up the New Testament is called "canonization." The New Testament canon was essentially agreed upon by the end of the second century, A.D.[5]

The church made decisions about which writings were to be recognized as scripture. Canonization, from a theological point of view, was the work of the church which sought to establish authoritative writings to serve as norms for faith

and practice. The Holy Spirit worked through the church
in such a way that certain writings were eliminated while
others became scripture. Biblical scholars Robert Spivey
and D. Moody Smith observe:

> Some early writings were eliminated because they were not
> the work of apostles or authors with apostolic connections;
> others fell into disuse or were considered less profitable,
> unsound, or even dangerous. Gradually a consensus
> developed on the need for a canon and on the books to be
> included in it. [6]

Actual canonization and agreement on the number
twenty-seven was not settled until the latter part of the
fourth century. [7]

Some people may find the discussion of the process of
scriptural canonization so new as to be profoundly
threatening. Many Christians have not thought carefully
about the actual process by which the Bible came into
being. It is important to understand that God works through
men and women in human community. The Bible is at
once a product of faithful community and a gift of grace to
that community. To affirm the role of human agency is by
no means to negate the essential reality of divine agency.

I began by affirming the priority of the church and
emphasizing that the church is not merely human
community, but is the divine gift of God. This affirmation
is the key to understanding what it means to say that the
Bible is the product of the church. Examination of the
process by which the books of the New Testament were
written and authorized leads to an approach to the authority
of the Bible which is theologically sound and practically
helpful.

What is the nature of the Bible's authority? Its authority is the result of *God's action* in which *God's Word* is revealed to *God's people*. The Christian canon, therefore, speaks with authenticity to a degree beyond comparison with other literature. Men and women have found in it the power to define reality, to change life patterns, and to redirect attitudes. It has been a source of strength and comfort in time of need as well as a harsh judge and prophet. So consistently has the Bible offered insights for theological reflection, resources for personal devotion, and guidelines for ethical prescription that some Christians have asserted the Bible to be the *unique* authority for thought and action.

Unique authority means that the pages of scripture contain the Word of God for all matters of belief and moral judgment. The advantage of such an approach to biblical authority is that it appears objective. According to this approach, Christians are not left with ambiguity about what they are to believe, but have an absolute standard, the Bible, by which all else can be judged.

The problem though is that the Bible does not offer such an objective standard. Based on the Bible claims are made for every sort of belief and action. This is so because the Bible does not speak consistently with one voice. It is a collection of diverse writings from diverse historical periods. It is possible to use the Bible to justify a wide variety of positions.

Some Christians make irresponsible claims. One example of this can be found in the newspaper, on Saturday, on the weekly church page. There one can find ads by churches whose ministers claim to preach the "pure unadulterated Word of God," or to engage in "straight Bible preaching." These slogans, of course, are designed to evoke emotional response. In fact, what does it mean to talk about the "pure and unadulterated Word"? Would the preacher simply read from the Bible without comment? *Someone* must *interpret* the Word. The task of preaching is interpretation.

The Word of God for men and women finds expression in *human* language. Human language is partial, it is not capable of carrying God's revelation in a complete way. If it were, we would have the full knowldge of God on earth, a knowledge which, in fact, is not possible in human terms. The wholeness of Christian truth cannot be contained in words. One who reads the Bible must bring judgment and insight to it. Also, the message of the Bible depends upon the continued action and presence of the Holy Spirit. The Bible does not speak directly to many matters in the modern world, but it can and does speak meaningfully through the interpretation and application of the Spirit at work in the church.

Perhaps a greater danger than insisting on the unique and absolute authority of the Bible is the contemporary tendency not to take the Bible seriously. The idea that scripture is the result of nothing more than subjective human activity diminishes its objective and authoritative character. The historical critical method of criticism, that arose in the late nineteenth century and became ascendant in the twentieth has made indispensable contributions to biblical scholarship. It continues to be an essential tool of Christian biblical interpretation. It can also contribute to a reduction of the Bible which, for the Christian, is theologically indefensible. Taken on its own terms, the Christian canon is inseparable from the Christian community which receives its validity from God.[8]

I have emphasized the dual character of the Bible. It is the product of faithful community, but it is more: God's work in community is such that we are required to talk theologically of scripture as the mediated Word of God for men and women. In this sense, human critical tools of biblical scholarship and interpretation must *themselves* come under the authority of the scriptures. Though the Bible is the first and most important norm of Christian faith it is not the only norm, and, in the context of Christian community, its truth is received experientially in relation to other historic norms.

2. *Church Tradition and the Shaping of Christian Faith.* Church tradition is a second authoritative guide to the meaning of the message of the gospel and the mission of the church. Church tradition includes the wealth of creeds, liturgies, polities, confessional writings, stories, ethical teachings, hymns, and characteristic uses of language which have proliferated in the course of the church's life.

Especially important in church tradition are the historic creeds of the church. The church tried to capture in brief summaries the most important elements of its faith. The great creeds were intended to exclude those interpretations of Christianity that the community declared to be "wrong teaching" (heresy).

The Nicene Creed, for instance, the product of the great Council of Nicaea (A.D. 325), declares that God was in Jesus Christ without any diminution of his sovereign deity. For the church, the presence of God was defined in Jesus Christ. The creed thus rejected the theology that made Jesus less than wholly God and, at the same time, affirmed the nature of God and the relation of God to Christ. The Nicene Creed is a statement of the faith of the church. As such, it is a starting point for theology, a norm for Christian doctrine.[9]

The Apostles' Creed and the Nicene Creed are preferred

to modern creeds because they are universally accepted by
Christians as authoritative. Modern creeds, which seek to
accommodate contemporary language and philosophical
preferences, may actually represent breaks with tradition.
The ecumenical Christian creeds are tests against which
our own judgments and understandings are measured.
They receive their authority from the community of faith
and in turn are authoritative for the community of faith.
They are both raw data and authoritative measuring tools
for faith and nurture.

Attention to church tradition is a conservative aspect of
the church's life. The church has a great deal to conserve;
in fact, the church is by nature and by necessity a
conservative institution. Without the riches of accumu-
lated experience we would have nothing against which to
test our immediate experience of God's grace and mercy.
Subsequent generations of Christians learn from the
communion of saints and judge contemporary understandings of individual and corporate Christian life against
the richness of the past.

It would be a mistake to make church tradition uniquely
authoritative. At times some Christians make this error.
The Roman Catholic Church, at certain periods in its
history, tried to absolutize church tradition. Even the Bible
was read through the eyes of tradition. The refusal of the
Catholic Church to ordain women, for instance, is an
example of absolutizing church tradition. The church does
not base its objection to women priests on scripture, but on
tradition.[10]

The Protestant Reformation recognized the mistake of
absolutizing tradition. It freed God's Word from clergy and
tradition in order that it could again be a living witness to all
men and women. But Protestants are not immune to the

mistake of absolutizing tradition. We all know persons who object to any change in the life of the church. Refusal to change is a rejection of the continuing power of the Holy Spirit to sweep through our communities with fresh winds of new life, new possibility, and new insight.

The most important questions facing the nature of Christian faith and the moral shape of Christian life need to be seen in light of tradition. Even more essentially, if tradition is one of the major norms of faith, then the church must attend to tradition as it lives its life. To be a Christian is to be accountable and that accountability includes the rich tradition the church perpetually inherits.

3. *Experiencing the Faith.* The recognition of experience as one of the norms of Christian faith refers not to the experience which accrues through living in the world, but to personal religious experience. Religious knowledge does not come to one simply through argument or learning. Religious knowledge includes a dimension of reality having to do with the affections. Some philosphers and theologians have referred to it as the "sense of the heart." The truth of the Christian theological affirmation that Jesus Christ is Lord and that Jesus Christ is God comes not through a series of rational steps leading to commitment, but through the gift of God's inexplicable grace. The immediate vitalizing reality of God captures the mind by capturing the "heart."

The revelation which comes through innerexperience, however, is not a wholly sufficient guide to faith, nor an adequate guarantee of authenticity. A woman, who had a "religious experience" that led her to become an active Christian, told me that all she believed was a result of her personal experience. Such a remark is not unusual, but it does suggest limited understanding.

The claim that experience is an all-sufficient norm for Christian faith and practice does not make sense for at least two reasons. First, such an affirmation is inadequate because, as we have noted, no one becomes a Christian in a vacuum. Other Christians, the Bible, stories, and reports from Christians who have gone before, pervade not only the church, but also, all Western culture. Christian allusions pervade literature and art. One of the remarkable developments in China today is the preparation of a book which will explain six hundred common references from the Bible and Christian experience so that Chinese students, unfamiliar with these allusions, can comprehend Western literature. So pervasive is Christian language and reference in the literature of the West that it becomes unintelligible apart from knowledge of things Christian. Psychologists have amply documented the fact that what we absorb unconsciously from our surroundings is translated in subtle ways into experience brought to consciousness. No one becomes a Christian wholly alone.

Second, we know that personal experience alone is not an adequate norm because our perceptions of experience cannot be fully trusted. Our experience must be tested against the experience of others. This is especially true of religious experience. The problem of discerning authentic religious experience is very great. We cannot presume that one's experience will be pure or true. Evangelist Oral Roberts reported that he had been visited by a nine-hundred-foot-high vision of Jesus. On the basis of his experience with the visitation, he was authorized to press forward with a hospital building project for his university. What is one to make of such a report? Is one to accept the report on its own grounds? To what extent does one need to account for a range of issues surrounding the report? Other

Christian norms need to play a role: Bible, traditon, reason. Modern psychology shows us that feelings, emotions, and passions are unpredictable and exceedingly complex. They need to be shared and tested.

Immediate experience of God is real and undeniable, moreover, for genuine Christian faith and practice it is essential. Experience comes in prayer, meditation, Bible study, reflection on life's purpose, and in communication and relationship with persons. The recognition, translation, and interpretation of such experience requires the help of other norms which God has given. The Bible, church tradition, and reason aid the Christian to discern authenticity in experience.

4. *The Rational Character of Christian Faith.* Reason in Christian faith involves the full use of the capacity of the human mind to understand the other norms and to stretch the limits of religious knowledge. At some points in Christian history trust in the rational capacity of human beings was such that reason was celebrated as the chief norm. The test of all religious claims was their ability to satisfy the human mind. Perhaps the idea of the supremacy of reason as prior to and independent of other religious authority had its most classic statement in the latter half of the seventeenth century when the French philosopher Descartes asserted that belief in God could be based on the self-evidence of reason. "It is Reason," he said, "that proves my existence. I think, and therefore, I am. It is in my Reason that I find the idea of God. My belief in Him rests neither on the authority of the Church, nor on the authority of Scripture, but on my consciousness of His existence."[11]

The idea of reason that Descartes set forth, and which dominated the successive generations of believers in reason, was essentially simple. It was thought that the human mind was capable of dispassionate, objective evaluations of reality and that this rendered it the absolute authority. This philosophical position, which was first advanced to "prove the existence of God," ironically sowed the seeds of profound skepticism in things religious. It was not long before "scientific enlightenment" predicted the ultimate end of religion because it could not stand the test of reason.

The human mind, however, is highly complex and subject to varieties of inexact impressions. Today one hears less often the classic argument that human reason can be objective. More subtle analysis is now required, because of a growing sense of the limitations of the human capacity to understand and control all things. In the early twentieth century some scientists, such as Andrew D. White of Cornell, predicted the end of religion, because they believed scientific advances would move men and women toward perfection. Today confidence about the ability of science and technlogy to "save" humankind is greatly diminished, perhaps completely gone. There is a new awareness, in all areas of research, that human reason has limits. [12]

In what sense, then, is reason among the norms of Christian faith and practice? The norm of reason requires that the Christian make use of every possible help that research, study, and thought can provide. In short, Christians are called on to use their brains, and the brains of others, including currents of thought, scientific advance, and artistic expressions that do not originate in Christian community. Christian faith calls one to a life of continuing growth. Life in Christian community is processional; there is perpetual movement toward fuller comprehension of

God's intention for the world. Ignorance has always been an enemy to true faith, because faith's conviction is that God's purpose and intention are ultimately shown in all things. Greater knowledge, then, harmonizes with faith. One of the greatest needs in the modern world is for the Christian community to advance vigorously again the claims of the unity of Christian faith and rigorous scholarship. Faith works against obscurantism. Reason is a norm, which, in concert with other norms, contributes to the process of determining what the Christian is to know and to do.

Authorization and Discernment: The Shape of the Christian Life

Prior to setting forth a Christian approach to professional practice, it is necessary to offer a way of thinking about Christian faith and the problem of the authorization of belief and action. At base is the Christian community. The priority of the community of faith is both a historical fact and a perpetual reality. The individual Christian self is shaped by, and in turn shapes, the community. To be a Christian is to be accountable to norms external to the self and its preferences. One of the serious errors in popular Christian thinking is a simpleminded emphasis on individual decision and action. We are individuals, and ultimately before God we are held accountable for what we do, but overemphasis on this theme can result in irresponsible individualism. We are accountable to God and to the church which mediates God's grace in the world. In the context of community, historic and living norms serve to authorize belief and action. These norms—

scripture, tradition, experience, and reason—are *mediators of God's grace.*

It is possible to indicate the way in which the multiple norms of faith, in the context of the community, actually function in the process of authorization. Often confusion in the church has been the result of wrong emphasis of one of the norms, or a partial combination of some of the norms. Affirmation of the multiple norms reminds Christians that there *are norms*, that the norms provide a *context of accountability*, and that they also celebrate the gift of *Christian freedom.*

In his Letter to the Philippians, Paul talks about growth in faith and in ability to perceive the will of God:

> I thank my God in all my remembrance of you, always in every prayer of mine for you all making my prayer with joy, thankful for your partnership in the gospel from the first day until now. And I am sure that *he who began a good work in you will bring it to completion* at the day of Jesus Christ. It is right for me to feel thus about you all, because I hold you in my heart, for you are all partakers with me of *grace.* . . . And it is my prayer that *your love may abound more and more*, with *knowledge and all discernment,* so that you may approve what is excellent, and may be pure and blameless for the day of Christ.
>
> (Phil. 1:3-7*a*, 9-10, my emphasis)

Two things in particular are to be noted in this passage. Paul suggests that the Christian life is a life of growth. It is God who begins a good work in a person and it is God who brings it to completion. Christian faith involves one in movement toward the goal of full life in God through Jesus Christ. This "fullness of living" might also be described as "eternal life," since eternal life is at once a reality for the

Christian in the world and a reality that awaits fulfillment. There is growth in Christian living; one finds this sense in Paul's prayer "that your love may abound more and more."

The Christian life is processional because its perpetual movement is not random, but specific. It moves toward the goal of full life in Christ. This is what John Wesley meant when he talked about "going on to perfection." God's grace initiates and sustains the growth. Grace is continuous from the point of beginning to the point of consummation. The Christian life thus literally begins and ends in God.

The processional character of faith defines the nature of the moral life. Being a Christian is neither to "fall back" nor to stay in a steady state (cf. Rom. 8:15). Accordingly Christian decision making takes place in growth, and this idea is applicable to diverse ethical problems and situations.

Paul suggests that growth in faith is related to "knowledge and . . . discernment." Knowledge derives from experience, observation, and instruction. Discernment allows one to apply knowledge following the norms of Christian faith. The image of the discerning person is useful for thinking about Christian living. To discern means to separate things mentally. It suggests the ability to sort through a complex situation in order to make sense of the whole. Discernment involves the process of ordering. To discern is to be able to "see" clearly, not necessarily in terms of seeing with the eye, but in terms of perceiving what is real, and coming to some conclusion about reality.

We speak, therefore, of the discerning person as one who can "see" or "read" the signs of the times. A person of discernment is able to make judgments that follow from the perception of differences among the multiple factors which comprise complex wholes. The word "discerning" suggests carefulness, and we use "discerning" as a positive adjective.

The shape of the Christian life is one of discernment. The Christian does not have a set of simple rules by which faith is translated into action, but neither is the Christian an independent actor who makes decisions by inclination or feeling. Christian faith rejects the juridical model that prescribes set laws for living. Doubtless there are rules that serve as plumb lines against which Christian action is to be judged. Perhaps most often such rules suffice, but they do not always serve. Even the Ten Commandments require interpretation. Christian faith rejects, as well, the dangerous idea that there are no guidelines external to individual conscience that guide thought and action. Faith rules out cavalier and undisciplined living.

Christian decision making is processional in that it involves movement through a series of steps toward the goal of authorized action. *Authorization derives from the process of discernment.* The norms of faith must each be taken into account. Discernment requires careful reflection on the relationship among the norms in a given case. The Christian person is called on to read scriptures in the light of tradition; the insights of scripture are tested in terms of experience; one must also seek to understand the process and arrive at conclusions that accord with reason. The individual does not engage in the process of discernment apart from the immediate vitalizing reality of God's Holy Spirit. Openness to the Holy Spirit informs and qualifies the process of authorization. This is not a model where, in the final analysis, the individual's evaluation is determinative. It is a model in which the multiple norms guide the process of discernment and, at the same time, require accountability.

By using the model of discernment to characterize the shape of the Christian life, I have emphasized the accountability and responsibility of the Christian person. It is now possible to put this model to work, in relationship with the idea of a profession, and with understanding of moral education and ethical analysis to move toward a Christian model of professional responsibility.

5

TOWARD A CHRISTIAN MODEL OF PROFESSIONAL RESPONSIBILITY

We have explored the traditional definition of a professional and some of the problems the definition faces in contemporary society. We have examined some of the particular problems of the learned professions and have suggested some guidelines by which Christian ethical thinking can be applied to problems of the professions. Now we need to set forth with clarity and precision a Christian model of professional responsibility.

Ethical Demands of the Professional Idea

The tasks performed by the professions are undoubtedly indispensable in any imaginable social order. Is it necessary, however, to perpetuate the idea that these task performers are professionals, and thus subject to a different set of standards, obligations, and privileges than any other contributors to the society? Does the title "professional" have any content and meaning? Would it be best simply to accept the fact that, in the modern world, the professional ideal is nothing other than a self-serving myth? Can anything else be concluded after more than a decade of Watergate lawyers, lawyers in Congress convicted of taking bribes, physicians embroiled in Medicaid scandals, and spiraling malpractice suits?

The fact that professionals do not always live up to the professional ideal is no reason to give up on the traditional definition and regard it as nothing but a self-serving myth. If we do this, we will lose the professions as we have known them and risk even poorer service because we will have lost the built-in ethical demands of the professional idea. I think it may be that the traditional idea of what it is to be a professional, if rightly communicated, can be a point of renewal. Professional men and women can be challenged to work to manifest the high standards demanded, by definition, of a professional. Ethical demands exist within the professional heritage. These ethical demands are rooted in the Western Christian tradition and are the result of the fact that the professions began within religious orders. A restoration of serious ethical sensitivity on the part of individual practitioners and leaders in the professions would result in untold benefits to American society and would answer much of the negative citicism that is plaguing the professions today. What I am suggesting is that serious attention needs to be given to the normative ethical demands that arise from the earliest conception of what it meant to be a professional. For Christian men and women, these demands shape the nature of professional practice:

1. The professional must manifest a *concern for persons*. The professions are involved in the greatest personal concerns human beings have. I suppose this point is obvious with regard to physicians who are serving patients, attorneys who are dealing with divorces, wills, and criminal trials, and clergy who are serving parish churches. I think it applies to men and women who work for corporations or institutions as well, if they are to regard themselves as professionals. A professional cannot ever allow the needs of an organization to hide the human dimensions of his or her activity.

Recently, I talked with an attorney who had been

employed by a corporation for seven years. The corporation manufactured a product that had not been properly tested and that resulted in serious injury and permanent disability to a number of persons. The attorney was assigned the job of defending the company's interests. His research convinced him the company had misrepresented the facts of the case. As he prepared the case, he talked with two of the young men whose lives had been altered when they used the product, a piece of industrial machinery, in their work. He was uncomfortable about using his brains and energy to defend his company against these men who, the attorney concluded, used the machinery according to instructions and yet were injured. He resigned and went into private practice. He told me that he could not reconcile his image of himself as an attorney with the use of his skills to act against those young men. He manifested a concern for persons by his recognition that he was unwilling to take some cases. He thus exercised ethical judgment and took the consequences which included, at least for a while, serious financial dislocation. A concern for persons is not, of course, in itself an adequate ethical guideline, but it is fundamental and defines a starting point for professional ethics.

2. A professional exemplifies a concern for *society as a whole*. True professionals care for the best in a culture; they concern themselves with values and efforts to attain excellence. This is not to say that professionals are an elite who are the only ones so charged; but it is to say that the large questions which are at the heart of any culture are central to the concerns of the professional. Professional people are those who have not only a broad base of liberal knowledge, but also a particular competence in an area of

special knowledge and a proven ability to unite their best thinking with strategic action to better serve society.

A free, democratic society needs to have within it men and women who care about issues that go beyond survival and deal with meaning and value. These persons need to be capable of defining the issues, articulating them clearly, and working through democratic processes to influence public policy. Increased specialization in their own disciplines on the part of professionals has reduced the amount of public service rendered by professional people. I was told recently by a pathologist that he had been asked to serve on a public service commission to evaluate his county's long-range road development. He refused, arguing that he knew nothing about roads and had no time to learn because his practice was so demanding.

Physicians are properly viewed as the most conservative professionals in America. As a whole, they tend to enter the public sector mainly to defend the prerogatives of their own profession. Some responsibility for this reality must be laid at the door of medical schools which set forth unrealistic demands. Some of it has to do with the heavy practice loads most physicians carry. To a certain extent the reputation may be undeserved. But the fact remains that physicians are capable of more disciplined service to the larger society and both the society and the profession would benefit. All professionals need to understand their practice within the larger framework of society's needs.

3. Within the traditional definition of a professional is the ethical demand that the practitioner exhibit a certain *selflessness*. I do not mean that the professional should exhibit no self-concern, to make such a suggestion would be foolish. A profession exists to serve people's needs both individually and communally. If needs are to be met, the

professional cannot cater exclusively to selfish desires. Not all professionals exemplify the ideal, but fundamental to being a professional is the willingness to put selfish interests behind a willingness to serve those who need what only the professional can provide.

4. Inherent in the idea of a profession is a *critical spirit* which prevents one from "becoming the profession." One of the pitfalls of professional education is the socialization that seeks to eliminate critical distance between the new practitioner and the profession he or she is entering. The late Carlyle Marney used to tell of playing golf with a prominent physician. One day Marney asked his parishioner what he was when he wasn't a doctor. "By God, I'm *always* an M.D." was the decisive reply. Unless one can maintain some distinction between one's profession and one's self, the capacity for evaluation and careful reflection is lost. Change and new developments within a profession result from a willingness on the part of some members of the profession to risk new thinking. Such thinking requires critical distance. It is an ethical mandate that one not become wholly associated with one's profession because to do so is to relinquish individual accountability. Ultimately the professional must exercise personal judgment. A critical distance requires the practitioner to arrive at judgments that are independent.

These four points demonstrate that normative demands emerge from the definition of what it means to be a professional. The normative demands are rooted in Christian understanding of the relationship between faith and daily life. This relationship can be articulated theologically in terms of *discipline, covenant,* and *collegiality.*

Accountability and Professional Discipline

I think it can be argued that self-discipline is the greatest need of the professions today. Professionals are not exhibiting intelligent self-regulation. Medicine and law, in particular, are guilty of rampant individualism to the extent that some Americans regard themselves as victims of the professions. Irresponsibility, with regard to fee structures, group discipline, and personal accountability, has resulted in calls for various forms of regulation. Such calls are the result of fervent convictions on the part of many that the professions cannot, or will not, regulate themselves. A major question for American society is whether the professions will once again be accountable to the needs and desires of the public without the imposition of external regulation.

Professional men and women are chiefly responsible for the current crisis caused by the distrust of professionals. The professions must attend to questions of self-discipline and corporate discipline. Every individual practitioner needs to examine the implications of self-discipline for his or her own work. It is the most important factor in the definition of a professional. Self-discipline includes a number of factors. It involves the elementary necessity of high standards and responsible use of time. It also includes such matters as examination of assumptions about reward systems. Professionals sometimes assume they deserve rewards which are out of proportion to the rest of society. Careful reconsideration of a system that equates professional service with wealth might offer substantial benefits to the professions. Both our historical definition and the Christian model toward which we are working suggest that only if a profession exemplifies real self-discipline, which is manifest to the larger community, are its rights and privileges *legitimate*.

Individual self-discipline is the least difficult concept for professionals to understand, although the implications of self-discipline for the reward system may be unpalatable.

Most professionals have been trained to be disciplined individuals. Only disciplined persons are able to compete successfully and persevere long enough to enter a learned profession. Most professionals continue this self-discipline in their careers. The self-discipline here proposed, however, goes beyond the individualism of task orientation to the larger questions of professional practice in a social order. Self-discipline also means restraint, and this is what many professionals find distasteful because they regard it as their right to be privileged. I am suggesting that the concept of discipline needs to be applied not only to the way in which skills are used in practice, but also, and equally importantly, to the style of practice and its impact on the society as a whole.

Not long ago, I was invited to lecture at a house staff meeting of a large hospital. The surgeon who was serving as president of the staff, and who was my host, warned me that a controversial issue would be discussed that evening at the meeting following my lecture. The issue involved the purchase of a computerized axial tomography scanning device (usually known as a CAT scanner) for the hospital. The cost of a CAT scanner is variable according to how sophisicated the instrument is. In all cases, however, the cost of a CAT scanner is so high, often up to $700,000 or more, that regional health planning commissions now often limit the number of CAT scanners in a given population center so that each instrument is used to capacity and unnecessary duplication is avoided. In the case of the hospital where I was lecturing, the regional planning commission was in the final stages of deliberation and it appeared to hospital administrators that the hospital would be allowed to purchase a CAT scanner so the house staff was being asked for a decision about the purchase. A serious complication arose when a group of private neurologists, who practiced at the hospital and whose offices were across the street, made an announcement at the meeting that they had signed a private contract to purchase a CAT scanner for their offices, a move which could be made without the approval of the regional health planning commission. The neurologists hoped, of course, that the hospital would now abandon its effort to acquire a scanner and use the one in their offices. Obviously the neurologists had moved entirely outside of the spirit of the regional planning commission, though they were clearly within the law. They stood to gain if the hospital did not move ahead with a CAT scanner. The other physicians realized the implications of this private group's action. It would not be to the benefit of the other physicians, the hospital, or the community to have the two CAT scanners across the street from each other, nor would it be beneficial to have one scanner in private offices. Nevertheless, when the proposal to purchase a CAT scanner for the hospital came to the floor of the meeting, no physician was willing to express what everyone knew: the contract to purchase a private CAT scanner was, in fact, a disregard for the well-being of the many. The meeting voted to table the matter and directed the president of the staff and the hospital administrators to examine the matter and report back.

This example is pertinent to a consideration of professional discipline because it illumines a number of issues. It is an example of the lack of self-discipline on the part of the neurological group. Presumably each of the neurologists exhibited discipline in the manner in which he practiced; yet together they were not exhibiting self-discipline but were using their power to purchase a private CAT scanner that would benefit them but would not be the best use of resources for the community as a whole. Here is a case where self-discipline could have prevented the abuse of professional power and privilege.

The interesting thing is that when the issue was before the house staff, no physician was willing to speak the truth they all knew so that the hospital could go ahead with the purchase of the CAT scanner. (Most of the physicians assumed that if the hospital did go ahead, the private group would not, evidence that the economic benefits to the neurologists would be assured only if they had an effective monopoly.) Here is a case where a group of physicians was unwilling to discipline some of their number even when the self-interest of the majority was at stake. The individualism that is emphasized in professional education makes professionals reluctant to discipline one another. This is the other aspect of professional discipline. The case of the CAT scanner combines two aspects of the issue. Self-discipline was not exerted by the neurologists. Tradition has it that professionals will police themselves. But, even in the case of their own self-interest, there is an overwhelming hesitance on the part of professionals to discipline one another when self-discipline breaks down. The prevailing opinion seems to be that an individual professional should be able to do what he or she wishes as long as it does not violate the law or some canon of professional ethics. Much of the criticism of professionals from lay men and women stems from their perception that, although the traditional

idea of a professional includes discipline for the sake of
those served, the reality often breaks down.

The Covenant Image of Professional Responsibility

The concern we have expressed for professional
discipline as fundamental to a Christian approach to
professional practice receives embodiment in the image of
covenant. Throughout history, the idea of covenant has
had both religious and legal aspects. Covenants have
reference to regulation of individual behavior. In the Old
Testament, for instance, the idea of covenant bound the
people of Israel to one another and to God. This binding,
when rightly understood, had practical behavioral consequences. To be a true child of Israel was to act in certain
ways which were predictable. As a result, the covenant
implied *trust*, *predictability*, and *accountability*. The New
Testament writers refer to Christian faith as a "new
covenant." The accounts of the Last Supper report Jesus'
words as announcing a "new covenant" between God and
human beings and among men and women which he
inaugurates (Matt. 26:28; Mark 14:24; Luke 22:20). The
"new covenant" is key to the development of the concept of
Christian community. Paul, for instance, speaks of
Christian leaders as "ministers of a new covenant" (II Cor.
3:6).

The Christian community is the standard of Christian
faith and practice and is central to a model of Christian
professional practice. The Christian is part of the body of
Christ and, as such, is a member of a community that has
claims on the self (I Cor. 12:27). Though the Christian
person is an individual created by God and has worth and
significance as a self, and as a self in relationship to God,

proper relationship to God propels one into relationship to the church. Relationship in the church involves the basic demand that the Christian relinquish selfishness. Perhaps the most difficult aspect of self-giving is allowing the Christian community to make and exert claim over one's life in the way Paul described: "If one member suffers, all suffer together; if one member is honored, all rejoice together" (I Cor. 12:26). The Christian professional is thus called on to modify behavior not simply according to a notion of legal right or wrong, but according to the reality and standards of the church. Individual preference and independence are subject to the good of the whole body of Christ (I Cor. 8, 9, 10; Rom. 14).

The Christian idea of covenant, then, involves the covenant relationship between God and the Christian self, but it also involves the relationship among Christian selves. Selfhood is qualified in relationship to other persons as it is qualified in relationship to God. This idea of covenant has significant implications for our concern with the idea of a professional. We have seen that the earliest notion of a professional was tied to Christian profession and service. Through the years, secularization and pluralism have mitigated the traditional notion of professional service to the point where the term "professional" has lost a great deal of meaning; or, perhaps more accurately has taken on a different set of meanings. All professionals might well contemplate the implications of the change in meanings and intentions. Christian believers who are, or intend to be, physicians, attorneys, ministers, or other professionals should give serious attention to the implications of a Christian view of professional practice. The hallmark of such practice is discipline, responsibility, and accountability within the context of Christian community.

The covenant image implies first of all that priority is given to community, rather than to the self and its goals. The strong voluntary character to the covenant image moves one away from regulation and requirement to a willing self-control in light of larger needs. In the case of the neurologists and the proposed CAT scanner, for instance, a Christian model of professional practice would require careful examination of the good of one's fellow professionals and the community as a whole. Individual action motivated by ends beneficial exclusively or primarily to the self would be qualified by the demands of the larger community. Even though the larger community, in a secular society, is not "Christian," the Christian professional is bound by the norms of the communal in such a way that the ends of self are put into the perspective of the larger good. A CAT scanner would serve the community and other physicians more effectively in the hospital than in the private-practice clinic. Therefore, the physicians could restrain themselves, and their colleagues could support that restraint so the hospital's claim would be protected. When this kind of self-discipline and discipline within the profession exists the community is better served. Such an ongoing process would protect the high standards of the professional ideal and would make outside intervention unnecessary. One could also imagine instances where responsible action would cause a hospital, or other institution, to stop undercutting private individual action.

Although the society as a whole cannot be expected to operate under a Christian model of professional practice, serious consideration of the role of the *Christian professional in a secular society* is needed. Commitment on the part of Christian professionals to resist easy accommodation to the dominant standards of individualism, self-aggrandizement, and greed in favor of self-discipline, service, and generosity would create real change in American society. Ironically, it would also mitigate demands for external regulation and control of the professions because professionals would be more fully approximating the professional ideal which, though tarnished, is not corroded beyond recognition.

The covenant model of professional responsibility also protects the professional person from one of the serious dangers that characterize the learned professions, namely, the tendency for the professional to be so serious about the *self-as-professional* that the *self-as-self* is lost. All of us know persons who are identified only through their profession. Professional school socialization makes this almost inevitable. Christian faith reminds us that our identity as selves comes not from the role we play in society, but from our relationship to God in Jesus Christ and, because of this relationship, from our participation in the Christian community which is the body of Christ. Our significance is as one member of the body, and our obligation is to seek the service of the body, as a whole. Our identity is not derived, then, from society but from our Christian identity. We are not named by virtue of the role we play, but we are named by our fundamental relationship to God. The covenant model strips us of pride that comes from allowing our professional identity to become the mark of our personhood. Only if one is freed from such bondage to the *self-as-professional* can one be freed for *self-as-servant*. The covenant model liberates the Christian professional to become a true self in the context of community.

The recognition that selfhood is derived from Christian identity, which is antecedent to professional identity, allows one to move toward a sense of mutuality not only with colleagues in a profession, but also with persons in other professions, who can be colleagues, and most importantly with patients, clients, parishioners, or whomever it is that one serves. Most often the image of the professional in American society is that of a person who has knowledge and skill that he or she makes available to lay men and women. It seldom, if ever, occurs to the professional that a layperson can help the professional. The image of professional invincibility is carefully calculated and cultivated. There is legitimacy to the image. No one needs a minister who is unable to "take charge" when there are pastoral needs to be met. Nobody needs a lawyer who appears uncertain about the nature of his or her expertise. On the other hand, if the professional's responsibility is to serve and equip others, then the one being served must be taken seriously as a whole person. Moreover, the covenant model would suggest that the professional might be helped by the one who is served. There is mutuality to all human relationship. A recognition of the personal benefits derived from such relationships can go a long way toward redeeming professional arrogance and pride.

The covenant image of professional responsibility unites a number of concerns mentioned in this book. The Christian professional is part of the community of the new covenant. As such, the individuality of the professional is qualified. This recognition can lead to professional practice which is excellent not only in terms of knowledge and skill, but also in terms of service and relationship.

PART
THREE

AUTHORIZING
CHRISTIAN
DECISION

6

ABORTION

The Traditional Dilemma and Contemporary Complications

In this chapter, it is my intention to use the problem of abortion as a case study in an attempt to demonstrate an approach Christian theological thinking might take with regard to a specific issue. One of the claims of Christian theology is that Christian faith has direct relevance to the way in which life is to be lived. It is the argument of this book that the Christian faith has implications for professional practice. In a time when pluralism is the spirit of the age, it is necessary for the Christian community to consider carefully the nature of Christian response to difficult problems and offer some guidelines for specific cases.

The problem of abortion offers an opportunity to explore the relationship between theological thinking, practical life, and professional practice. There certainly is no question that abortion is a problem and is recognized as such by thoughtful people. This is so because abortion is not simply a matter of private, personal response between a woman and a physician, but a matter of public policy. As such, abortion is perhaps the most emotional issue facing the United States.

Abortion is a major political issue because of the strong sentiments expressed about the proper social policy

response to it. Some people think the government should
have no part in the decision of whether or not a woman has
an abortion. Such persons believe that the matter is a
personal one, between the woman and a physician. On the
other hand, others think that abortion is murder and should
be banned by the government. Such persons seek an
amendment to the Constitution to prohibit abortions in the
United States. Their argument is that abortion is a public
issue and should not be left to the decision of an individual.
Many others have differing points of view in between these
polar opposites.

Political action groups whose sole purpose is to influence
governmental policy concerning abortion have become a
potent force in American politics. Persons who profess the
Christian faith are prominent in many political action
groups concerned with abortion. What are we to make of
this significant disagreement among Christians? How are
Christian decisions to be authorized? Are such decisions
merely individual? Or is the Christian to seek authorization
beyond the self?

I have argued in this book that Christian life is
processional, rather than static. We do not, therefore, have
a reservoir of certain rules from which we can get absolute
answers to specific problems. Rather, the life of the
Christian is lived in relationship with the Christian
community, whose initiation is the result of God's action.
In relationship with God, and with God's community, we
are able to respond to the particularities that confront us.

Abortion is a problem which unites the concerns of
medicine, law, ministry, philosophy, ethics, and theology.
This is so because it deals with one of the most profound
mysteries, the nature and meaning of human life. For the
Christian professional dealing with this important issue, it

is necessary to understand the problem and think about the *process* by which a Christian might deal with it.[1]

Let me identify briefly the diversity of concerns with the problem:

The Medical Situation

Physicians are able to terminate pregnancy with a number of surgical procedures that are statistically safe.[2] Yet traditionally many physicians have been unwilling to do this operation without extensive counsel, deliberation, and satisfaction on their part that failure to do so would result in the death of the mother. Often physicians were forbidden by law to perform abortions, except in emergency situations. Furthermore, many physicians were reluctant to deal with the problem openly. Perhaps this is so because it was regarded as different from other surgical procedures and therefore, as a whole, considerably more complicated, and perhaps even beyond their expertise.

The medical situation is complicated by the fact that prior to the 1973 Supreme Court decision, which will be discussed later, large numbers of women sought and received abortions. If they were not able to get them from reputable doctors in modern hospitals, they sought and received them through the underground connections of illegal abortionists and many of them died.[3] Virtually all physicians would agree that if abortions are to be performed, they should be done in a setting that assures the greatest potential for the survival and the well-being of the mother.

Abortion is more than a medical problem. Procedures are clear and relatively safe. Settings that maximize the safety and well-being of the mother are possible. Some physicians will perform an abortion for any woman who seeks one. Regulation and certification of such services are possible for the protection of the patient. The individuals in the medical profession are no different from other people in society; their responses to the problem of abortion are manifold.

The Legal Situation

In twentieth-century America, until 1973, state law governed abortion. Generally state statutes forbade abortion except in the case of extreme danger to the mother's health or in the case of felonious sexual intercourse, such as rape. Even in this case laws were not liberal and the definition of rape, as the women's movement pointed out, is unclear and difficult to prove legally.

In the 1960s, there was a variety of proposals to change state statutes regarding abortion. Various constituencies, bar association panels, church groups, and political action committees proposed legislation.[4] Several states adopted liberalized abortion laws, notably Colorado, North Carolina, California, and New York. These laws permitted abortion if it was necessary to preserve the life or health (specifically including the mental health) of the mother, if the pregnancy resulted from rape (including statutory rape and incest), or if there was a substantial risk that the baby would be born with a serious physical or mental defect. The New York law was the most liberal, and in that state abortion could easily be attained legally.

The diversity of state laws governing abortion created understandable problems. A national policy was needed to obviate the inequities and inconsistencies among the states. The United States Supreme Court finally accepted a Texas case, known as *Roe vs. Wade*. The ruling in that case was issued on January 22, 1973; and it is that ruling which currently prevails (*Roe vs. Wade*, 410 U.S. 113).

Associate Justice Harry Blackmun, representing the seven-to-two majority, ruled that, because of the right to privacy guaranteed in the Fourteenth Amendment, a woman has a constitutional right to an abortion at least for the first trimester of a pregnancy. In the second trimester, states could enact legislation dealing with medical procedures used for abortion, but could not limit the reasons for abortion. In effect, the Court's ruling meant that for the first six months of pregnancy, the decision to abort was left to a woman and her physician. In the final trimester, the period traditionally thought of as "viability," when the fetus could exist apart from the mother, a state could forbid abortion, except in the case of danger to the mother's life.

Roe vs. Wade became one of the most celebrated Supreme Court decisions in history, eliciting widespread opposition and support. It may also be one of the most far-reaching Supreme Court decisions in history. By striking down the right of a state to proscribe abortion in the first two trimesters, and limiting the reasons for such proscription in the last trimester, the Court made it possible for virtually any woman to obtain a legal abortion in the United States.

Historically, abortion has also been a problem in legal theory. Legal theorists have pondered the point of "viability" of the fetus. That is, at what point does the fetus attain the status, for legal purposes, of a human being? Common law tradition has suggested that "quickening," the point at which an infant is felt by the mother, is the time when "rights" begin. Notice, however, that both legal theory and legal rulings respond to the needs of society to regulate its common life. The point is that abortion is a legal problem because society recognizes a problem that requires adjudication beyond the individual.[5]

The Political Situation

In the 1980s, abortion emerges as a critical political issue in America. Though medical and legal matters are involved, they are secondary to the moral question. Medical and legal matters do not determine, and can never determine, whether or not abortion is "right" and therefore should be "legal." The nature of the political situation is not difficult to understand.

In opposition to the prevailing norm, which was established by the Supreme Court and which provides legal abortions for women who elect them, a large group of Americans seek to outlaw abortions. The earliest and most vocal leadership of the movement to make abortions illegal came from the Roman Catholic Church. It is wrong, however, to think that opposition to abortion is limited to, or even primarily made up of, Roman Catholics. The national movement is an interesting mix of Christians, Orthodox Jews, and advocates of conservative politics, who may, or may not, have religious reasons for their objection to abortion. The strongest Protestant opponents of abortion are Evangelicals and Fundamentalists.

The people who think that any abortion is wrong want an amendment to the Constitution of the United States forbidding the practice. If a constitutional amendment is passed, it will overrule the Supreme Court decision. Though the constitutional amendment is probably a long way off, the issue is very much before Congress. Efforts are already underway to begin the process. In the meantime, opponents of abortion in Congress have succeeded in passing legislation that prohibits the use of federal money, in the form of Medicaid payments, for abortions.[6] This makes it more difficult for a poor woman to get an abortion. However, it does not affect the situation for those who can afford to pay. When he was questioned about this inequity, President Jimmy Carter remarked, "Life is unfair."

Another effort of the "right-to-life" movement is to pass a bill called the Human Life Statute which seeks to undercut the *Roe vs. Wade* decision by defining the initiation of life as the point of conception. Such a definition would mandate that the unborn fetus is guaranteed the right to life by the Fourteenth Amendment to the Constitution. Thus Congress would define the point of life's initiation, a definition the Supreme Court declared itself unable to give. The Human Life Statute proposes a political answer to a question that has been unresolved by medical, legal, philosophical, and theological debates. The wisdom of such a political attempt is as controversial as the question itself.

It is clear that significant political gains have been made by those who oppose abortion. A politician's stance on abortion has become, in some cases, the determinative issue in elections. Block voting on the single issue of whether or not a prospective congressman or senator would seek a constitutional amendment prohibiting abortion has removed some people from office and helped others succeed.[7] Without a doubt the National Right to Life Committee is a potent political force.

Opponents of abortion have adopted the phrase "right to life" to identify their cause. Accordingly to them, a woman does not have the "right" to supersede the "right" of the unborn to live. It is, therefore, murder; and murder cannot be tolerated in a civilized society.

Large numbers of people do not agree with the effort to forbid abortion. The prevailing opinion, at least officially, in the United States, is that abortion is a matter for the individual to decide.[8] The issues and circumstances are so complex that to offer a categorical ruling would not do justice to the subtleties inevitably present. The "pro choice" movement is also a complicated mixture of persons representing the religious community, especially main-line Protestant churches, women's rights groups, civil liberties groups, and other Americans who think that it is unwise to try to impose a law about which there is so much difference of opinion. The crisis for the United States in the abortion dilemma is that the nation's lack of shared values is becoming clear in a way that has not been clear before.

The heated, and sometimes vicious debates, accusations, and pronouncements which are a part of the political process concerning abortion have shaken the nation. There are many nuances of the problem. From a personal and psychological point of view, continuing studies seek to understand the impact of abortion on the individual woman. From a philosophical point of view, thinkers ponder the impact of abortion on a society's sense of the value of human life. What does it mean, for instance, for a society when one-third of all pregnancies end in abortion, which is now the case in the United States where over one-and-a-half million abortions are performed annually?[9]

Serious questions from a world-wide perspective are also raised. Most of the nations of the world regard abortion as a means of population control. One need only reflect for a moment to see the relationship between world population growth and birth control and abortion. The problems of world hunger cannot be ignored and will make increasing claims in coming years. Any discussion of abortion must also deal with the reality that at all times and in all places abortion has been done; abortion has always been available to those who had the motivation, information, and money.

Abortion is a major social issue for the 1980s because it involves medical, legal, philosophical, political, psychological, and sociological concerns. It is also an issue that has a theological tradition. Precisely because it deals with some of the most complex matters of human life, abortion has always been a major concern of religion. I will now turn to an examination of abortion in the context of Christian theology. Abortion will be a case study for the approach to Christian accountability I proposed in chapter 4 and to the model of professional responsibility suggested in chapter 5.

The Theological Tradition

Throughout its history, the predominant thinking of the Christian church has considered abortion to be wrong. This is so despite the fact that the Greco-Roman world, in which Christianity was born and took root, largely accepted abortion as a means of birth control. Both Plato and Aristotle approved of abortion before "quickening"; this extant philosophical justification might have been adopted by Christianity. But Christianity received its primary convictions about the God-given character of human life and the importance of children from its Jewish heritage. Children were a gift from God and greatly to be desired. The Old Testament scriptures suggest that to be childless is to be less than complete; and a marriage without children is a failure.[10] The patriarchal character of Judaism, moreover, made it particularly desirable for a man to have male heirs. A man's status was determined in part by the number of children he had; and, after his death, his heirs provided family continuity. This was important because the family was the source of identity in relationship to God as well as in relationship to human community. For this reason, obligation to future generations, the faithful community yet unborn, was taken seriously.

Judaism's regard for marriage, children, and openness to new life derived from its theological conviction that the world, and all that is in the world, are the products of God's creative power. God was active not only in the life story of Israel, but in the story of the whole of creation. Israel's theological genius connected the history of a particular people to the history of the world. Israel's God was also God of the universe; and God was the giver and sustainer of all life. Life, particularly the mystery of new life, was to be protected and celebrated. Any prohibition of the procreative potential in marriage, therefore, was rejected.

The *Didache*, among the earliest Christian writings, expressly rejected abortion as early as the beginning of the second century A.D. Christianity distinguished itself sharply over against the dominant culture. Virtually all the early Christian fathers specifically prohibited abortion as an option for the Christian person. To be a part of the Christian church was to be set apart from the moral values and actions of the regnant society.

The Christian church, from its beginnings in Judaism, regarded the procreation of children to be a natural part of God's perpetual creative process. Indeed Christian thinkers came to recognize God's law in the natural order. (An early example of this is Romans 1:18*ff.*) An understanding of the relationship between God's intention and the world's reality known as "natural law" developed. The idea is that God's will is manifest to men and women in the natural order of the world. Human beings, as creatures of God, are not to inhibit the natural order because to do so is to disobey the will of God.

The natural law theory became a basis for Christian approach to human sexuality. Accordingly, sexuality is a natural biological function directed toward the procreation of human life. Marriage is the God-given state in which children are welcomed into the world. For this reason, sexual intercourse outside of marriage is regarded as sinful because intercourse might produce children and children are to be born only into a marriage. Within marriage children are always possible, and nothing is to be done to interfere with that natural possibility. It is this theological understanding of the natural law which caused the church to reject artificial means of birth control. Birth control is interference with God's natural order.

Abortion is unthinkable in the natural law tradition because it is direct interference with the natural development of human life. The birth of a child is a gift from God to be welcomed and celebrated. The human disposition to reject such a gift is contrary to the will of God and is, therefore, sin. Abortion is to take into human hands a power that belongs only to God, namely the giving and taking of the mystery of human life. Such usurpation of power upsets the natural order of the universe because the creature seeks to replace the creator.

In Western Christianity, the Roman Catholic Church is the chief advocate of the natural law in theology and ethics. Roman Catholic opposition to birth control and abortion is best understood in the context of the natural law tradition. The consistency of interpretation and application of the Catholic position results from the idea that sexual intercourse belongs exclusively to Christian marriage, that children are the natural result of marriage, and that nothing should be done to prevent or terminate pregnancy.

Protestant thought has also rejected abortion, though usually for different reasons, and with less consistency. Protestant theology approaches humankind and the world in a different way from Roman Catholic theology. The Catholic approach is to avoid intervention in natural processes because God's will is worked out in them. Protestant thinkers regard humankind as invested by God with responsibility for the world. This does not mean that, in the final analysis, God is not in control. Rather it means that men and women are called on to use their God-given brains to make the world a better place in which to live. Men and women are thus partners with God in the improvement of the world as agents of ongoing creation.

The result of this Protestant approach has been an impetus toward economic and scientific advancement in the name of human progress. Western European and American Protestantism provided a theological foundation for scientific research and experimentation. This spirit of inquiry provided an approach that allowed new discoveries to be thought of as a legitimate part of, indeed, a potentially significant contribution to, God's world. If God is sovereign Lord of all creation and if men and women are creatures of God, then new discoveries can be understood as contributions to the good of the whole. New ideas, and applications of new ideas, are, therefore, not to be feared, but to be welcomed and explored as gifts of God.

This theological foundation contributes to the development of medical advancement. It helps explain why Protestant theologians can respond to birth control in a positive way. At one time disease, natural disasters, and relatively short life spans meant that world population was not a problem, but changing conditions have made population trends a major concern. A characteristic Protestant approach is to be open to new ways of thinking about population control and to advocate intervention in the natural process in order to curb population growth and make the world a better place. Protestant theology seems to justify human intervention in the natural order. So much has this been the case, in fact, that it is possible to suggest that some of the ecological problems of the modern world are the result of sophisticated men and women trying to improve on nature.

Fundamental to Roman Catholic theology is the idea that there is "right teaching" and that the church is the institution on earth through which God communicates that "right teaching." Accordingly, authorized teaching concerning abortion is both possible and necessary. Most Protestant theology is reluctant to assert absolutes of ethical action. The absolutes of Protestant assertion have to do with the essentials of Christian affirmation, such as the reality of God, the nature and work of Jesus Christ, and the grace of the Holy Spirit. When pushed, a theologian of Protestant persuasion will always affirm that, in the final analysis, only God is God. This means that men and women cannot know, with *absolute* certainty, that a given *specific* action is wrong. I have already explored the serious problem of authority that results from this approach; and I have also noted that the problem now is not limited to Protestants. Even in the case of abortion, a number of Roman Catholic moral theologians are proposing some modification of the traditional absolute prohibition.[11]

According to this approach, it is not possible, even in the case of abortion, to assert that in every case, and without exception, abortion is wrong. To admit an exception, of course, is to open the door to all manner of speculation and reflection. That is why the question of abortion is such a difficult one to deal with theologically, and almost impossible to deal with politically and legally. Subtleties do not lend themselves to political rhetoric. The difficulty of the challenge should not, however, force the Christian church into silence or resignation. The question now before us is the way in which the specific problem of abortion can be dealt with in terms of the multiple norms of Christian faith through the process of Christian discernment.

Abortion in the Context of the Multiple Norms

I have suggested in this book that authorization of Christian belief and action comes through a process in which the Christian person, in the context of Christian community, is accountable to the norms of Christian faith. The whole of Christian life is processional in character. This processional character means that we are constantly growing in relationship to God and to one another. Christian life and belief are not static. To be a Christian is to be radically open to the formative guidance of the Holy Spirit. We are stripped of our easy certainties and previously learned responses, even as we are buttressed by, and accountable to, the ancient affirmations of the faithful community of which we are a part. The processional character of faith also means that we are moving toward a goal we have not reached. That goal, which is full life in Christ, draws us on and restrains us from bogging down in the mire of our own limits.

Such an approach to life and faith is not easy. It is much

easier to have positive answers. No doubt many Christians seek absolute pronouncements precisely because they are comforting in a time of change and uncertainty. But what is easier does not matter; all that matters, finally, is faithfulness as we stand before God. Men and women cannot have the certainty that God's will is unequivocally known in a given way. The possession of such certainty is not within the capacity of humankind. To be human is to be limited in all things.

The Christian person is part of a community which, as I have emphasized earlier in this book, is both human and divine. The church breaks in on the singularity of the Christian person to qualify the individual's belief and action. The essential idea is that the Christian cannot think of moral action as individual response. It is that in part, of course, but to be a Christian is to recognize the limited nature of one's individuality. Because the community is the principal arena of God's presence and action, it is there that response is shaped. The norms of Christian faith are gifts of God to the church, and they can be understood and used only in the context of the church. Let us, then, consider the problem of abortion in terms of the multiple norms from which authorization can be discerned.

The Bible. The scriptures of the Old and New Testaments do not mention abortion as such, and so it is not possible to turn to the Bible for a simple prescription. Rather, the Bible directs us to a style of life that points toward what is important and, therefore, what is to be valued.

The Bible is clear in its affirmation that all of life is a gift of God. This is what the Genesis creation narratives are all about. For the Jew and the Christian, life is not thought of as accidental or incidental. Life is sparked by divine intention, and for this reason it has meaning and purpose. The affirmation that life is the gift of God causes faithful persons to speak of human life as "sacred."

When biblical faith supports the value and sacred character of life, the reference is to more than biological life. Jesus, for instance, talks about losing one's life for his sake in order to realize it (Matt. 10:39). The Christian life is not dependant on earthly life alone. Eternal life involves a relationship with God which transcends the limits of the worldly. The New Testament expresses a concern for the quality of life; life in Jesus Christ involves human relationship characterized by qualities such as communal interest, loving spirit, spiritual depth, and compassionate advocacy (Rom. 8; Phil. 1:27; II Cor. 4:18; Gal. 5:22; I John 4:10-21).

I am saying that though the Bible does not offer a simple answer to abortion, it does provide authoritative directions for consideration of the matter. The most essential direction it provides has to do with the sacred quality of human life. No Jew or Christian can take the mystery of the initiation of life lightly. Moreover, for the Christian, God actually became incarnate in human life as Jesus Christ (John 1:14). That incarnation tells us that human life was good enough for God. In Christ, God became human; henceforth, humanity can never be the same because in every man and woman one can see flesh and blood like that which hosted God. The overwhelming sense of the sacredness and awful beauty of human life leads faithful persons to abhor the idea of taking life for any reason.

Tradition. In considering the tradition of Christian thinking, we emphasize the idea that moral decision making is not and cannot be a totally individual process for the Christian. As Christian persons, we are part of a community which has a history of thought about abortion. Consideration of abortion in our time requires us to take note of the fact that throughout Christian history there has been an overwhelming hesitance to terminate life, and an almost absolute prohibition of abortion.[12]

At the same time, the church has justified the taking of life in certain instances. One thinks of the "just war" theory in which the church permitted killing by Christian soldiers.[13] Elaborate qualifications concerning war do not mitigate the fact that the "just" nature of a given war depends, in part, on the point of view of the church at the time, and for this reason pacifist Christians have denied the rightness of any killing. Pacifists have never been dominant in the church, however, and the realities of human problems have resulted in efforts to approximate biblical intentions.[14] Some Christians have justified capital punishment as a legitimate means of taking another's life, and some have defended killing another person in an act of self-defense. Christians have always affirmed the sacred character of human life and rejected the taking of life, but they have recognized times when killing could be justified.

The tradition of the church includes within it recognition that scripture and tradition are to be interpreted in relationship to each other. The interpretive task, which has been part of the life of the church in every time and place, mediates between moral absolutes ("thou shalt not kill") and practical reality ("The fugitive would have killed four persons in the house had not the policeman killed him first; therefore, we justify the policeman's act, even as we regret its necessity").

Official Roman Catholic thinking about abortion is that interpretation of scripture and tradition prohibits abortion. This position is consistent with the refusal to intervene in the natural process where initiation of life is concerned. If, on the other hand, one thinks of a case where interpretation of scripture and tradition could justify abortion, then a whole new approach to the question would be required. Thus the church might take on the difficult interpretive task of abortion as it does for other forms of killing. The issue is not when life begins, but whether life should ever be taken. I do not think it is helpful to debate the question of the initiation of life.[15] The idea that before a certain point "life" has not begun and, therefore, abortion is justified strikes me as unconvincing. Christians need to recognize clearly that abortion is, by any theologically meaningful definition, termination of life. Church tradition does include the possibility that, in some instances, the taking of life, while regrettable, is morally justified. Such a conclusion is difficult, and has many ramifications; but Christians are called, before God, to deal faithfully with complex and difficult problems.[16] The Christian community must, however, keep before it the fact that church tradition has always recognized human life as a direct and holy gift of God. Life is to be valued and preserved; it is to be taken only in the most special case, and then with profound sorrow.

Reason. Men and women are created rational creatures. We are called on to use our capacity for reason in the difficult decisions we have to make. Reason is not the sole norm of Christian faith, but Christian faith does not require us to give up reason. The importance of this norm for the discussion of abortion is that the complexities of the contemporary situation for Christians, and for the society in which the church exists, require that sophistication inform ethical recommendation and action.

Reason requires that the church recognize that not all cases of abortion are the same. Christian evaluation of the decision to abort will vary with the particulars of the case. A number of factors are pertinent to every case which contribute to the total reality. The conditions and ways in which the woman became pregnant, the family situation, and the medical prognosis, are but examples of relevant variables.

Reason, as a norm of Christian faith, reminds us that we cannot responsibly avoid the realities at hand and act as if we lived in a perfect world which is not subject to complicated inconsistencies and manifold variations.

Experience. The experience of God's presence and grace in our lives permits us to accept the burden of decision. Living in the world, persons have to make difficult decisions; but the love of God is sufficient even for the awful decisions persons have to make, and some professional persons have to make regularly. These include, for example, the decision to abort, or the decision not to do radical surgery on a seriously impaired newborn in an attempt to maintain biological life. Indeed the experience of God requires and allows the Christian to live fully in the world accepting the risks and difficulties of unpleasant demands. Men and women are not paralyzed with the burden of fear and guilt because God has given the freedom to make a mistake in the light of God's love.

God alone is the absolute sovereign Lord of life. No other absolute is possible for men and women. The wonder is that while God is absolute, God is also gracious. The Christian recognizes this grace as that which works in one prior to anything one does in relationship to God. God's love is total and serves as the spark of life and the perpetual regenerator of life.

The capacity for the experience of God's grace is fundamental to human life. Human life, therefore, is to be protected and preserved. The experience of God's love is total, however, and not dependent on the reality of physical human life. God's love enfolds the living and the dead. The mystery of eternal life is that it is both now and in the future. Eternal life is a quality of life that transcends human understanding and can be affirmed, but not explained.

Recognition that there are *norms* of Christian belief and action is an affirmation that the Christian person is *accountable beyond the self.* I have suggested the image of a *discerning person* as useful for thinking about the *process of authorization.* This approach offers help in the case of abortion. The multiple norms of scripture, tradition, experience, and reason function for the Christian person in the faithful community to enable the process of moving toward authorization for decision. The norms work together to require the recognition that, in a specific instance, mature Christian discernment might conclude that abortion is justified. To say this is not to open the door to a selfish, abortion-on-demand mentality. I have carefully qualified this discussion in an attempt to make it clear that I am not talking about abortion as a means of birth control or abortion as an "easy out" for an indiscreet sexual mistake which resulted in an unwanted pregnancy.

The alternative to the approach suggested in this chapter is to say that there is no case in which abortion can be judged "right" from a Christian point of view. To make such a statement would be to assert an absolute certainty contrary to the mediation of God's Holy Spirit in the norms of faith. It should be clear from what I have written that a Christian person could not easily elect or recommend abortion. But it is also necessary to say, from a theological point of view, that breaking the prohibition against abortion might be right. If the process of discernment required the awful decision of abortion, then the decision is authorized not by individual whim, feeling, or inclination, but within the context of Christian community and within the experience of God's enveloping love.

This discussion is suggestive for consideration of social policy. The church has an obligation to the society in which it lives to teach and to recommend. At the same time, the church must recognize that the Christian community is not the same thing as general society. The church can and should participate in the general society by attending to the crucial issues about which it cares. Abortion is, obviously, one of these. In what ways can the church, and especially the professional practitioners who are part of the church, seek to influence the society on the matter of abortion?

A constitutional amendment forbidding abortion is an attempt to impose an absolute moral judgment in an area of complex and subtle realities. Christian faith does not require the assertion that abortion can never be right. For this reason, from a Christian theological point of view, the effort to enact a constitutional statutory absolute is unwise.

It is unwise also from another point of view. While Christian faith might wish to require moral obedience to its standards, the translation of such standards to the general society is difficult if not impossible. This is especially so in the case of abortion, where serious differences of opinion exist among Christians. The constitutional amendment, encouraged by Christians, that made the sale or use of beverage alcohol illegal in the United States did not work because large numbers of people in the society did not agree with the absolute moral judgment. Accordingly, while liquor did not disappear, an elaborate system of illegal means for the procurement of the illicit drink did appear.[17]

A constitutional amendment to ban abortion would not make abortion disappear, but it would cause untold numbers of illegal abortions to be done in settings often not conducive to the health and well-being of the women involved. An amendment outlawing abortions but allowing for exceptions, such as cases of rape, incest, or medical problems, would result in extraordinary complications and require complex bureaucratic machinery to operate. Such consequences need to be considered by Christian people.

Church concern about abortion further suggests a need for self-examination on the part of the Christian community about the kind of witness it is making to the society on the whole matter of human sexuality. Christians understand human sexuality as a gift from God. As with all God's gifts, sexuality requires responsibility. Sexual responsibility is particularly critical when there is the possibility of conception. Accordingly, planning for parenthood must be one of the preeminent concerns of the Christian community. While the moral standards of the church derive directly and specifically from its theological vision and commitment, concern for the potential child can be shared with the general society. Renewed attention to education about birth control is required because of the relationship between birth control and the painful reality of abortion. I share the traditional teaching of the church that intercourse belongs exclusively to Christian marriage. I further think that family planning should precede any possibility of conception. But any professional person who has dealt with unplanned and unwanted pregnancies knows that these moral mandates are not the prevailing norms in contemporary society. Concern and compassion for the unwanted child and for the parents dictate attention to birth control along with teaching about responsible sexuality.

Human sexuality is an instance where the church cannot effectively impose its moral standards on the general society by law; the church must convert the world to its moral vision by example and persuasion.

Abortion is an unpleasant reality. It is one of the ugly realities with which men and women have to contend because we are human and therefore capable of figuring out how we can have some control over our lives. God has given us this capacity. Dealing with the results of our human development is part of the burden of Christian living. The resources of the Christian faith, particularly the multiple norms within the context of the Christian community, provide meaningful and realistic help for the struggle. The mistake is to think that the answers are simple.

7

SEVERELY HANDICAPPED CHILDREN

Severely handicapped children present the professions with a special constellation of issues. For medicine there are questions about the use of new technology, decisions about giving or withholding care, and concern about research directions; legal problems involve conflict of rights, professional and personal obligation, and private versus public goods; for theology there are theoretical questions about the relationship between mental and physical capacity and humanness, questions of the relationship of God's grace to human capacity, and practical problems of ministry to parents and children. Indeed, for the Christian professional person and the Christian community, severely handicapped children provide an almost unsurpassed challenge because they demand sophisticated tools of technology, rigorous legal evaluations, thoughtful theological study, and compassionate action in relation to persons who are not able to represent themselves. Severely handicapped children are wholly dependent on others, and, as such, are poignant reminders that our human condition involves limits of capacity for us all. I have chosen severely handicapped children as the topic for this last chapter because consideration of them brings together the theological, professional, economic, technological, medical, legal, and social policy concerns of this book and also, and most especially, because I think that severely handicapped

children provide an occasion for important theological
reflection.

New Problems from New Technology: Ultrasonography and Amniocentesis

Among the most remarkable developments in modern
medicine are the technological achievements that make it
possible for physicians to know the condition of the fetus
while it is still in the mother's womb. Doctors are now able
to assure thousands of anxious women and men that their
babies will be whole and healthy. Others can be warned of
problems that could make the birth difficult, or require
extensive care. Some learn that the fetus is significantly
damaged and likely to die shortly after birth or will be
unable to develop and live normally. Two techniques, in
particular, ultrasonography and amniocentesis, have
revolutionized the way in which obstetricians deal with
problems in prenatal care.

Ultrasonography was perfected during the decade
between 1960 and 1970, years of extraordinary technical
development in medicine. The process involves the use of
ultra-high frequency sound waves, well above the human
hearing level, which can be translated into a visual image.
Ultrasonography is noninvasive and, according to the best
current evidence, is devoid of any risk to the mother or to
the fetus. The test produces a picture of the fetus in the
womb, including tissues that cannot be seen on an X-ray.
This process allows the physician to learn about the
amniotic sac, to foresee potential handicapping conditions,
and to know the exact position, size, and condition of the
fetus. In cases where the fetus is normal, such information
can be helpful in alerting the doctor to special needs at the

time of delivery or the likelihood that a Caesarean delivery will be necessary.

Amniocentesis is a technique for learning about the fetus by inserting a long, hollow needle through the mother's abdomen and the wall of the uterus into the amniotic sac. This piercing of the amnion allows the doctor to take a sample of the fluid surrounding the fetus. Analysis of this fluid yields a great deal of information about the developing child. Obviously the dangers in an invasive technique like amniocentesis are greater than those in a noninvasive technique like ultrasonography, but current studies indicate the risks are small. If amniocentesis is prescribed, physicians usually suspect that some problems could be present. The test is often indicated if there is a history of genetic disorder in a family, if a previous child exhibited problems, or if ultrasonography indicated a need for further testing.

Tests can be done on the amniotic fluid for a number of conditions which affect the life and health of mother and child. Pigment analysis can demonstrate Rh incompatibility, for instance, and blood transfusion can be given to the child prior to birth. More seriously, certain proteins in the amniotic fluid indicate neural tube defect, a failure of the spinal canal to close properly. One such defect is known as spinal bifida and affects more than eight thousand babies born each year in the United States.

The amniotic fluid also contains fetal skin cells which make possible karyotyping, or chromosomal analysis. Such analysis informs the physician of the child's sex and indicates the presence of severe genetic irregularities, such as Down's syndrome, once known as "mongolism." Down's syndrome involves varying degrees of mental retardation and potential disorder of other organs.

Phenylketonuria (PKU), a defect of protein metabolism, which can result in severe mental retardation, and Tay-Sachs disease, a disorder of lipid metabolism, which is always debilitating and often fatal, are also detectable by amniocentesis.

Without question ultrasonography and amniocentesis are significant technological achievements in prenatal care. Through their use many men and women are relieved of unfounded fears. Also, in some cases, prenatal therapy can save the life of the child. At the same time, they present new problems. A host of complicated issues arise when it is possible for physicians and parents to know about the condition of a child before birth. Once the results of the tests are known, a series of decisions have to be made. On the one hand, the decisions may involve determination of whether or not to elect therapy for the fetus *in utero*. In such cases, the problems may be corrected or significantly improved. On the other hand, the decisions may involve the painful question of whether or not to elect an abortion. The moral questions are important because they have to do not only with the feelings of the individuals involved but also with the values of the entire society.

Some physicians insist that patients agree to abortion ahead of time if the results of amniocentesis indicate severe problems. How severe must problems be before abortion is indicated? Whose analysis of the situation is to be accepted? Not long ago I counseled with a Roman Catholic woman whose family had a history of genetic disorder. Her obstetrician wanted her to have amniocentesis; and she agreed to undergo the tests. At the same time, she was unwilling to contemplate an abortion under any circumstances. Her physican was then unwilling to go ahead with the tests even though she wanted to know the condition of the fetus prior to birth. As I talked with her, I could understand both her feelings and her doctor's judgment.

Now parents and physicans can make decisions about whether or not a certain child should be carried to term on the basis of information about the potential physical and mental capacities of the child. An example was recently presented in a case of a forty-year-old woman who was carrying fraternal twins and had not previously given birth. Because of her age, she underwent amniocentesis which indicated that one of the twins was normal while the other evidenced the genetic condition associated with Down's syndrome and potential physical defects. The woman asserted that she did not want the handicapped child because she "could not face the burden of caring for an abnormal child for the rest of her life."[1] The physicians, therefore, proposed to abort the abnormal fetus in a complex operation using ultrasonography to locate the tiny beating heart so that a needle could pierce it to withdraw half of the fetus' blood, thus killing the unwanted child. The report celebrated the technical excellence of the medical technology and the considerable skill of the physician.

This case is dramatic because it juxtaposes a potentially normal child with a potentially abnormal child and demonstrates the capacity for modern medicine to permit decisions such as that made by the woman "who could not face the burden" of an abnormal child. Several questions may be suggestive of the wide-ranging implications of the case: Does elected pregnancy (the woman had wanted to become pregnant) carry with it responsibility to accept the risks of pregnancy? What is the extent of abnormality that justifies killing the fetus? What values are involved when a normal child's life is preserved while a retarded child's life is destroyed? What are the long-range effects on a society which permits, even encourages, decisions to be made individually and justifies them on the grounds of personal preference ("she couldn't face the burden")?

The ambiguity of technological advances in medicine, and in most other fields, is that such advances result in notable benefits even as they present new problems. The new problems often go to the core of the values that sustain the social order. The Christian community needs to ponder its response to the capacity for such decisions and to the values that inform them.

Problems in the Neonatal Nursery

In 1973, Dr. Raymond S. Duff and Dr. A. G. M. Campbell contributed an article to the *New England Journal of Medicine* which was among the first discussions of the serious moral dilemmas that arise in special care nurseries with babies who are severely handicapped.[2] Duff and Campbell wrote that during the thirty-month period in which they did their study at Yale-New Haven Hospital, forty-three infants in the intensive care nursery were allowed to die because essential treatment was withheld. The children were hopelessly ill, congenitally deformed, or both. The decisions were made by parents and physicians acting together. The significance of the article is that it brought to light, in a systematic way, a reality that numerous professional persons must deal with regularly. Each year thousands of babies are born so severely deformed or seriously ill due to congenital disorders that they are almost certain to die unless extraordinary means are employed to keep them alive. The withholding of extraordinary means is acquiescence in their death.

In some cases infants are so clearly deformed that there is no hope that even with corrective surgery they will live. More difficult cases are those in which extensive surgery or life support systems might sustain life for an indefinite period. One of the children in the Duff and Campbell study, for instance, had chronic pulmonary disease, an incurable lung disorder; he was kept alive only by treatment of high oxygen concentrations. By the time he was five months old, he still required 40 percent oxygen in order to live. Nevertheless he had a bad heart and great difficulty breathing. He could have lived for some time, but he could not live without the high concentration of oxygen and the prognosis was grave. Duff and Campbell write:

> The nurses, parents and physicians considered it cruel to continue, and yet difficult to stop. All were attached to this child, whose life they had tried so hard to make worthwhile. The family had endured high expenses (the hospital bill exceeding $15,000), and the strains of the illness were believed to be threatening the marriage bonds and to be causing sibling behavioral disturbances. Oxygen supplementation was stopped, and the child died in about three hours. The family settled down and 18 months later had another baby, who was healthy.[3]

A number of years ago, I was called to the hospital late at night when a young woman in the congregation I was serving gave birth to a child who was seriously deformed. The spinal cord had not formed and the baby was without a back. From the front, the baby looked normal, but there was virtually no hope that the child would survive. Nevertheless, the physicians and parents were confronted with the question of whether to attempt surgery or do nothing. I talked at length with the pediatric surgeon, the couple, and the grandparents. After agonizing thought and prayer, the decision was made not to subject the child to surgery which would likely prolong physical life but would not permanently correct the multiple disorders the baby suffered. Any decision not to take every conceivable means to protect and prolong life goes against the ingrained normative thinking of modern medicine and culture. It is easier not to face such difficult questions, but, as Duff and Campbell observe, "pretending there is no decision to be made is an arbitrary and potentially devastating decision of default."[4]

A more difficult situation involving a decision not to undertake surgery on a newborn child occurred in the famous Johns Hopkins Hospital case in which a male infant, who was diagnosed as having Down's syndrome ("mongolism"), also had an intestinal blockage. He was allowed to die because the parents refused to give permission for the surgery which could have corrected the blockage (duodenal atresia). The child was separated from other newborn children and allowed to starve to death since feeding him, due to the intestinal blockage, would have killed him. In this case, the fact that the child was mentally retarded was the determinative factor in the parents' decision not to permit surgery. The intestinal blockage could have been corrected and the child could have lived.[5]

Consideration of decisions concerning newborn defective infants is related to previous discussion of ultrasonography and amniocentesis. If, indeed, one could consider the possibility of a genetically indicated abortion as the result of tests following amniocentesis, then one might not consider it an obligation to the severely defective newborn to use every conceivable means to prolong physical survival. The logic of moral accountability suggests that prenatal and postnatal obligation to the infant is similar, if not identical. The problem has to do with the point at which human action is appropriate and the extent to which intervention is justifiable. Is there ever a point, for instance, when genetic defectiveness is severe enough to justify termination of a pregnancy? To what extent should extraordinary means be used to sustain the physical life of a newborn, and how far do the legitimate research needs of modern medicine go in trying new methods on children who appear to be hopeless cases? Doctors Duff and Campbell report a remark made by a house officer to a research physician studying one child's disease, "For this child, don't you think it's time to turn off your curiosity so you can turn on your kindness?"[6] That remark demonstrates the fact that, even apart from religious language or affirmation, human sensitivity cries out for the recognition that there are conditions of physical life, perhaps "living death," which are worse than death. Christian affirmation, as we have seen in this book, because of its recognition that wholeness of living, or eternal life, is both now and not yet, can see how kindness might involve allowing the hopeless child, whose existence really serves only research, to die.

Some people insist that the answer to the difficult questions of human intervention or nontreatment of defective newborns is to use every conceivable means to preserve and protect life. The reason for this, they argue, is that once consideration is given to a question such as the quality of life, the possibility for error, misjudgment, or active malevolence is introduced.[7] In fact, nontreatment may involve the withholding of ordinary care, the withholding of effective but expensive forms of extraordinary care, or even, passive or active forms of euthanasia. The problems are significant and should not be hidden;

they cannot be solved by suggesting that human beings have
no business making such far-ranging decisions.

The same kind of advanced medical developments that
complicate pregnancy cause complications in the neonatal
nursery. Just as it is possible for sophisticated technology to
provide information that requires men and women to make
decisions about the fetus in the womb, so it is that
technology and advances in surgery make it necessary for
persons to decide whether or not certain mentally and
physically handicapped children should survive. It was
no doubt simpler when such capacity did not exist, but
ability now renders such decisions, though awesome,
unavoidable.

Legal and Social Policy Implications

Should judgments concerning severely handicapped
children be the exclusive province of parents and
physicians? Sometimes the courts get involved and are
called on to make decisions when differences of opinion
exist. In the Johns Hopkins case cited above, the decision to
let the child die was made by the parents; the physician did
not seek a court order to do the surgery which would have
saved the child's life. The physician pondered, after the
incident, what the effect of a court order would have been
in that case, or what it would be in any case, where
objections from the parents were rejected. Discussing the
difficulties of court-ordered treatment which goes against
parental preference, the doctor commented, "I think one of
the great difficulties, . . . is what happens in a family where
a court order is used as the means of correcting a congenital
abnormality. Does that child ever really become an
accepted member of the family? And what are all of the

feelings, particularly guilt and coercion feelings that the parents must have following that type of extraordinary force that's brought to bear upon them for making them accept a child they did not wish to have?"[8]

A thirty-year-old woman gave birth to a little girl who suffered from meningomyelocele, a disease that paralyzes the victim below the waist and sometimes causes brain damage. The prognosis was that she would live about two years. After consultation with medical specialists, the parents decided not to permit surgery that would arrest the disease and allow her longer life. Physicians and the hospital sought and won a court order to require surgery. The operations were done and the likelihood is that the child will live six to eight years. The lawyer for the parents commented, "They are loving, caring parents. Is it not the right of the parents to decide the course of their child, or is it the courts?"[9]

Do parents have the right to decide about the nature and extent of medical treatment for their children? The courts often intervene where physicians argue that parental-directed medical care is inadequate or wrong. One thinks, for instance, of court tests of parental rights in electing unorthodox methods of cancer treatment for their children. In the case of severely handicapped children, the issues are usually more complicated because of the emotional conflicts that exist for both parents and physicians. These conflicts stem from the fact that historically the handicapped often have been rejected, or judged to be of less value than those other persons. Even in the case of the "right to life" the issues are complex since, despite what one might wish, some severely handicapped infants are doomed to a "life" that counts for life only in the most simple biological definition.

A free democratic society does not, in fact, give to individuals absolute rights to decide what is best for them or their families. One of the themes of this book is that individualism carried too far is contrary to the good of the community. It is necessary to use legal means so some decisions concerning important ethical issues can be tested and adjudicated by persons not directly involved. So, decisions concerning severely handicapped children cannot belong exclusively to parents or physicians. The society has a legitimate concern that its values and principles be upheld. At the same time, as the Johns Hopkins physician recognized, legal action introduces a host of problems for all parties involved. Daniel Callahan was writing about abortion, but his observation applies to virtually all matters of ethics and the professions: "Nothing in our society has so muddied the ethical issues as its tendency to turn ethical problems into legal matters."[10]

Granting the legitimacy of legal intervention in particular cases of special complexity, it may still be suggested that the American proclivity to translate ethical dilemmas into legal proceedings can have negative consequences for professional practice. Legal categories, by nature, cannot handle the subtleties and particularities of some cases. If ethical formation is a part of professional education, and if professional persons recognize the ethical implications of the idea of a profession, the hard decisions, which all professionals inevitably encounter, usually will be made in the context of professional practice rather than in the context of legal arbitration.

In addition to legal issues concerning severely handicapped children, pressing social policy matters deserve attention. One is economic. Popular American thinking has accepted the assumption that medical care necessary for the protection and preservation of life should be provided regardless of cost. Confronted with an emergency operation, neither physicians nor patients generally engage in protracted consideration of the value of the operation in terms of a cost-benefit analysis. If a procedure is required to save a life, that procedure is used regardless of cost. This popular assumption, which has never been an entirely accurate reflection of reality, is now being examined by persons concerned about social policy issues and health care. It is now possible to keep alive many people who previously would have died. Some are destined to live a kind of "living death," wholly dependent on elaborate life-supporting machines. Some mentally and physically handicapped infants are saved for a life of institutional care, but are incapable of even minimal human interaction (let me be clear that there are some physically and mentally impaired persons who are capable of meaningful human interaction).

Economic realities now dictate that society ask some hard questions, and reach some decisions about the use of limited financial resources for medical purposes. Modern medicine is capable of keeping alive large numbers of persons who could not live without complex technology. The cost of intensive medical and institutional care is enormous. Often a large portion of the cost of such care is borne by public funds, since the amount of money involved soars beyond the capacity of private families. In the case of severely handicapped children who have been kept alive but who are incapable of living at home, social costs for these children will go on for years as the society helps to pay, or pays entirely, for their necessary institutional care.

Some years ago, Ross Laboratories of Columbus, Ohio, held a conference on "Ethical Dilemmas in Current

Obstetric and Newborn Care." In a startlingly honest appraisal, economist Richard E. Hatwick commented on the economic impact of modern medicine's capacity to preserve the lives of infants who, under different circumstances, would die:

> It is obvious from the data presented at this conference that the expenditures of large sums of money for intensive care could save the lives of many infants who would ordinarily die without such care. However, some of these infants will be mentally and/or physically handicapped. The care which a society must then provide for those that are handicapped forces substantial costs on that society over and above the costs for intensive care. These additional costs may exceed the benefits of saving the infants' lives in the first place.
>
> I am not suggesting that we should stop trying to save the lives of these infants. I am suggesting that the extent to which our society spends its money to do so be kept in perspective. After all, it is possible that the benefits achieved by the expenditure of monies allocated for intensive care will be less than the benefits that would accrue to the expenditure of the same money in other health care areas.
>
> While some may find the economist's viewpoint repelling, its virtue stems from the fact that it recognizes what none of the other disciplines seems to recognize, EVERYTHING HAS ITS PRICE. To ignore the cost is to make a decision to use resources in areas which may not be deserving of them. [11]

Dr. Hatwick's remarks are startling because of the bold way in which he applied economic analysis to the problem of severely handicapped children. Perhaps the greatest value of his economic analysis is its reminder that modern scientific and technological advances are making economic considerations an inevitable part of decision making. Certain medical procedures, organ transplants, for instance, are so expensive that serious questions will have to be raised about relative cost, access, justice, and legitimacy. At some point, the society will have to consider limitations imposed by finite resources.

Christian Discernment and Handicapped Children

Christian discernment helps the believer recognize that painful moral choices are those made not between what is good or bad, but between competing goods. To allocate resources for one purpose, for instance, prohibits their being used in another way. In a time of limited resources, a Christian might conclude that, as a matter of social policy, preventive and primary care medicine is the preferred use of resources rather than intensive care medicine for patients who have no hope of living apart from extraordinary life-supporting technology. Noting the kind of economic analysis provided by Dr. Hatwick, it is important to understand that the norms of Christian faith would not permit economic considerations to be determinative. Christian response to the social policy problem of limited resources for medical care would not be based on the argument that one life is more valuable than another. From a theological point of view, the value of life cannot be calculated in human categories.

Christian faith affirms that wholeness of living, or eternal life, means that Christians are not desperately tied to the limitations imposed by biological life. Christians seek to preserve and protect life in the world, but this intention does not become the *singular goal*; the singular goal is relationship with God in wholeness of living. It is in light of these faith and value considerations that Christian moral thinking might approach the complex and difficult matters of the allocation of resources for medical care. Mere biological existence is not wholeness of living and, therefore, if resources are limited, they might best be used to maximize the potential for persons to receive preventive and general care.

Our discussion of allocation of limited resources demonstrates the way Christian theology and practice go together. Theological thinking will reject economic, biological, sociological, or psychological determinism, for instance, but must still deal with hard questions in a realistic manner. One would prefer not to make such choices, but human capability and finite resources make choices necessary. Choices require norms; there must be some principles of choice by which decisions are made. For the Christian, difficult decisions, like those we have been considering, are made after reflection on the fundamental meaning of human life in light of the norms of faith.

Christian response to severely handicapped children is determined by the evaluation of human life in the context of faith. The norms of faith, as this book has suggested, make it clear that human life, because it is God-given, is precious and therefore to be preserved and protected. The nature and purpose of human life is relationship with God and other persons. These relationships have to do not with mental capacity, but with the depth of human personhood. A mentally handicapped person, though limited in mental, and perhaps physical, ability, may nevertheless be capable of relationship with other persons and, *because of God's initiating grace*, with God. Therefore, according to any meaningful theological definition, severely handicapped persons are no different than any other human being in value or potential, because the measurement belongs to God alone.

A Christian Approach to Professional Practice

A Christian approach to professional practice involves self-conscious identification with, and participation in, Christian community. It requires recognition of the norms of faith affirmed by the church and understanding of Christian decision making as a process. Christians are not simply individual actors; they are accountable to the community for their decisions and actions. Christian professionals practice in response to their prior and primary profession of faith. Practice is Christian faith lived according to the gifts and achievements of particular knowledge and applied expertise. This conception of professional practice offers a vision of commitment and service which can provide a recovery of the vitality lost as the professions increasingly are perceived as bastions of selfishness and privilege.

Being faithful means that one's values and priorities are set not by the limited vision of human reality, but by the vision of eternal truth glimpsed by Christian community. This vision determines one's understanding of what it means to be human. To be human is at once to have limitless potential, because of God's promise and relationship, and, paradoxically, to be profoundly limited. This limitation is often forgotten in modern culture as persons become overly impressed with human capacity. Persons are most dangerous when they think they can do anything, when they forget the true character of humanity.

This essential Christian vision is the key to Christian

professional practice. It reminds the professional person that he or she is accountable to God and to the Christian community for the fulfilling of vocation. It also provides a perspective that allows professional persons to see their vocation in relationship to God's larger purpose. In spite of all the modern technical capacities which give men and women the ability and obligation to make difficult decisions concerning themselves and others, human beings are limited. Nevertheless, God both requires and permits the freedom for men and women to decide and to act. A Christian approach to professional practice begins with God and God's grace. This approach relativizes all else and provides perspective that gives life its true meaning.

NOTES

Chapter 1

1. The literature is extensive and includes studies that examine the professions in general and that concern themselves with a specific profession. See, for instance, William J. Goode, Robert K. Merton, and Mary Jane Huntington, *The Professions in American Society* (New York: Russell Sage Foundation, 1957); also, Kenneth S. Lynn, ed., *The Professions in America* (Boston: Beacon Press, 1965).

2. See, for example, Wilbert E. Moore, *The Professions: Roles and Rules* (New York: Russell Sage Foundation, 1970), pp. 5-6.

3. For further consideration of status and the professions, see Amatai Etzioni, *The Semi-Professions and Their Organization* (New York: The Free Press, 1969) and Everett C. Hughes, *Men and Their Work* (New York: The Free Press, 1958).

4. For an analysis of professional consciousness and education, see Christopher Jencks and David Riesman, *The Academic Revolution* (Garden City, N.Y.: Doubleday & Co., 1969), pp. 199-256.

5. Samuel P. Huntington, "Power, Expertise and the Military Profession," in Kenneth S. Lynn, ed., *The Professions in America* (Boston: Beacon Press, 1965), pp. 131-53.

6. For a discussion of professional style, see Hoyt P. Oliver, "Professional Authority and the Protestant Ministry: A Study of Occupational Image" (unpublished Ph.D. dissertation, Yale University, 1967), pp. 64 ff.

7. See the report in the *Chronicle of Higher Education*, April 9, 1979, p. 2.

8. Howard M. Vollmer and Donald L. Mills, *Professionalization* (Englewood Cliffs, N.J.: Prentice-Hall, 1966).

9. See Thomas R. McDaniel, "The De-Professionalization of Teachers," *Educational Forum* (January 1979), 229-37.

10. For a discussion of professional education, see Robert Ulich,

Professional Education as a Humane Study (New York: The Macmillan Co., 1956).

11. The report of the Proceedings of the Inter-Professions Conference makes this point from a perspective of practice. See *Education for Professional Responsibility* (Pittsburgh: Carnegie Press, 1948), pp. 45-47.

Chapter 2

1. See Robert T. Handy, *A Christian America—Protestant Hopes and Historical Realities* (New York: Oxford University Press, 1971).

2. Peter L. Berger, *The Sacred Canopy* (Garden City, N.Y.: Doubleday & Co., 1967), pp. 107-11.

3. H. Shelton Smith, Robert T. Handy, Lefferts A. Loetscher, *American Christianity* (New York: Charles Scribner's Sons, 1960), Vol. 1, pp. 123-26.

4. The statistics on physicians are from a report of two American Medical Association economists: Gerald L. Glandon and Jack L. Werner (Chicago: Center for Health Services Research and Development, 1980).

5. Statistics and interpretation are derived from *Law Schools and Professional Education* (Chicago: The American Bar Association, 1980).

6. See Jackson W. Carroll and Robert L. Wilson, *Too Many Pastors?* (New York: Pilgrim Press, 1980).

7. See, for instance, his article "Can Ethics Be Taught?" *Change* (October 1976), 26-30.

8. *Newsweek* (February 26, 1979), 57.

9. For more on this issue, see William J. Bennett, "Getting Ethics," *Commentary* (December 1980), 62-65.

Chapter 3

1. James M. Gustafson makes this point in his essay "Education for Moral Responsibility," in Nancy F. and Theodore R. Sozer, eds. *Moral Education* (Cambridge: Harvard University Press, 1970), p. 11.

2. For helpful explanation and analysis of the "American democratic faith," see Ralph Henry Gabriel, *The Course of American Democratic Thought* (New York: Ronald Press, 1956).

3. The term "hidden curriculum" comes from the work of Lawrence Kohlberg and his colleagues. See, for instance, Lawrence Kohlberg,

with Phillip Whitten, "Understanding the Hidden Curriculum," *Learning* (December 1972), 194-97.

4. See Sidney B. Simon, "Values Clarification vs. Indoctrination," *Social Education* (December 1971), 902-5. Also, Louis Raths, Merrill Harmin, and Sidney B. Simon, *Values and Teaching: Working with Values in the Classroom* (Columbus, Ohio: Charles E. Merrill, 1966).

5. Lawrence Kohlberg, "Moral Stages and Moralization: The Cognitive-Developmental Approach," in Thomas Lickona, ed., *Man, Morality and Society* (New York: Holt Rinehart & Winston, 1976).

6. For a satisfactory overview of the major approaches in the moral education movement, see David Purpel and Kevin Ryan, eds., *Moral Education . . . It Comes with the Territory* (Berkeley, Ca.: McCutchan Publishing Corp., 1976).

7. The Hastings Center Report on the state of applied ethics in higher education and professional education is contained in a series of nine monographs which were published by the Institute of Society, Ethics, and the Life Sciences, Hastings-on-Hudson, New York, 1980. A summary report is contained in Daniel Callahan and Sissela Bok, eds., *Ethics Teaching in Higher Education* (New York: Plenum Press, 1980).

8. For a discussion of character and its relation to Christian practice, see Stanley Hauerwas, *Character and the Christian Life: A Study in Theological Ethics* (San Antonio: Trinity University Press, 1975). The shape of the Christian life in theological terms is discussed by David Baily Harned in *Faith and Virtue* (Philadelphia: Pilgrim Press, 1973).

9. The relationship between ethics and religion has been explored by James M. Gustafson in his book *Can Ethics Be Christian?* (Chicago: University of Chicago Press, 1975). He elaborates on the independence of ethics from theology in his essay "The Contributions of Theology to Medical Ethics" (Marquette University, Theology Department, 1975).

10. For a discussion of these matters see Christopher Lasch, *The Culture of Narcissism: American Life in an Age of Diminishing Expectations* (New York: W. W. Norton & Co., 1979).

11. *De principiis* 3,3,2. Quoted in Jean Danielou, *Origen*, trans. by Walter Mitchell (New York: Sheed & Ward, 1955), p. 41.

Chapter 4

1. Quoted by Janet Flanner in *London Was Yesterday* (New York: Viking Press, 1975), p. 92.

2. Letters, 51-55:24. See Williston Walker, A *History of the Christian Church* (New York: Charles Scribner's Sons, 1959), p. 92.

3. *The Book of Worship for Church and Home* (Nashville: The United Methodist Publishing House, 1964), p. 12.

4. One finds varying dating proposals. Those I have given are agreed on by most scholars. For an introduction to the dating problem, see Robert A. Spivey and D. Moody Smith, *Anatomy of the New Testament*, Second Edition (New York: The Macmillan Co., 1974), pp. 63-71. Bishop John A. T. Robinson recently set forth the argument that the New Testament writings actually were written earlier than is now generally assumed. His book explores in detail the dating controversy. See *Redating the New Testament* (Philadelphia: Westminster Press, 1976). Robinson's conclusions are not held by most biblical scholars. For a review essay on the matter see D. Moody Smith, "Redating the New Testament?" *The Duke Divinity School Review* (Fall 1977), 193-205.

5. For a discussion of these matters see Joseph B. Tyson, A *Study of Early Christianity* (New York: The Macmillan Co., 1973), pp. 27-30.

6. Robert A. Spivey and D. Moody Smith, *Anatomy of the New Testament*, second edition (New York: The Macmillan Co., 1974), p. 66.

7. Clyde Manschreck, A *History of Christianity in the World* (Englewood Cliffs, N.J.: Prentice-Hall, 1974), p. 7. See also Williston Walker, A *History of the Christian Church* (New York: Charles Scribner's Sons, 1959), p. 50.

8. The idea of canon is an important theological concept which has not been as central as it should be in biblical theology and systematic theology. A contribution to thinking about the canon in Christian faith has been made by Brevard Childs. See his book *Introduction to the Old Testament as Scripture* (Philadelphia: Fortress Press, 1979). Also his book *Biblical Theology in Crisis* (Philadelphia: The Westminster Press, 1970). See also Hans von Campenhausen, *The Formation of the Christian Bible*, trans. by J. A. Baker (Philadelphia: Fortress Press, 1972).

9. John Leith provides an introduction to the history and theology of the major Christian creeds in his book *Creeds of the Churches: A Reader in Christian Doctrine from the Bible to the Present* (Atlanta: John Knox Press, 1973).

10. Krister Stendahl shows that it is church tradition and not the Bible

that has been problematic for the ordination of women in his book *The Bible and the Role of Women* (Philadelphia: Fortress Press, 1966). See also Emily Clark Hewitt, *Women Priests: Yes or No?* (New York: The Seabury Press, 1973). Joan Morris, *The Lady Was a Bishop: The Hidden History of Women with Clerical Ordination and the Jurisdiction of Bishops* (New York: The Macmillan Co., 1973).

11. *Essential Works of Descartes* (New York: Bantam Books, 1961), p. 59.

12. Andrew D. White's collected lectures entitled *The Warfare Between Science and Theology in Christendom* were published in 1896. The lectures exude utter confidence in the capacity of humankind to perfect itself. Recent studies of the relationship between science and religion provide points of initiation for critical dialogue. See Ian Barbour, *Issues in Science and Religion* (Englewood Cliffs, N.J.: Prentice-Hall, 1966), and *Myths, Models, and Paradigms: A Comparative Study in Science and Religion* (New York: Harper & Row, 1974), also J. Robert Nelson, *Science and Our Troubled Conscience* (Philadelphia: Fortress Press, 1980).

Chapter 6

1. A useful overview of the entire matter of abortion is provided in a collection of essays edited by Joel Feinberg, *The Problem of Abortion* (Belmont, Ca.: Wadsworth Publishing Co., 1973). See also two books by Lawrence Lader, *Abortion* (Indianapolis: Bobbs-Merrill, 1966), and *Abortion II* (Boston: Beacon Press, 1973). An outstanding historical study of great importance to understanding abortion in America is James C. Mohr, *Abortion in America: The Origins and Evolution of National Policy, 1800–1900* (New York: Oxford University Press, 1978). Prior to 1900, abortion was legal in the U.S. Physicians took the lead in seeking to outlaw it and were aided in the battle by the clergy. Opposition to abortion was an effort to eliminate the scandalous practices of unprofessional abortionists.

2. All surgical procedures involve risk. Statistics from the former Department of Health, Education and Welfare demonstrate that the death rate of women undergoing legal abortions in hospitals and clinics was 3 per 100,000 in 1977. For the same year, H.E.W. estimated the death rate for women who had illegal abortions without the benefit of certified hospitals or clinics to be 50 to 150 per 100,000. Thus the safety of abortions is dependent upon the conditions under which the abortion

is performed. Under conditions of certified hospitals and clinics, abortions are as safe, or safer than other surgical procedures.

3. Statistics for abortions prior to 1973 are difficult to assess since no records exist for the thousands of abortions that were performed illegally. The Alan Guttmacher Institute of New York reports that, in the year prior to the 1973 Supreme Court decision, 744,600 abortions were recorded. The illegal and unreported abortions carried with them a risk of death estimated by the H.E.W. in 1977 to be seventeen times greater than those done legally in hospitals or clinics.

4. For examples of the arguments, see Alan F. Guttmacher, ed., *The Case for Legalized Abortion Now* (Berkeley: Diablo Press, 1967).

5. See D. T. Smith, ed., *Abortion and the Law* (Cleveland, Ohio: Case Western Reserve University Press, 1967).

6. "Federally financed abortions have all but ended; they have dropped from 295,000 [in 1976] to 2,400 in 1979." *Time* (April 6, 1981), 23.

7. For defense of single-issue voting in the case of abortion, see Grover Rees III, "The True Confession of One One-Issue Voter," *National Review* (May 25, 1979), 669-78.

8. By prevailing opinion I mean the only opinion which legally counts, that of the 1973 Supreme Court Decision, *Roe vs. Wade*. Polls sampling public opinion suggest that a majority of Americans agree with the Supreme Court decision. A 1974 NBC News poll "found that 58 percent of the voters questioned (and 46 percent of the Roman Catholics) approved of laws permitting abortion during the first three months of pregnancy—or wanted them liberalized." *Newsweek*, March 3, 1975, p. 19. By 1981, the percentage approving the Supreme Court decision had increased slightly: "ABC-Harris polls indicate that by 60 percent to 37 percent Americans approve of the Supreme Court decision legalizing abortion." *Time* (April 16, 1981), 26.

9. The Alan Guttmacher Institute of New York reports that in 1973, 19.3 percent of all pregnancies ended in abortion. In 1979, 30.3 percent of all pregnancies ended in abortion. In 1979, total reported abortions were projected at 1,540,000 in the U.S.

10. A major theme of the Old Testament is the value of children, and particularly the value of a son. The writers reflect this attitude in the stories of God's promises to future generations and in accounts of familial expectations. See, for example, Genesis 18.

11. See, for instance, Bernard Haring, "A Theological Evaluation," in John T. Noonan, Jr., ed., *The Morality of Abortion: Legal and Historical Perspectives* (Cambridge: Harvard University Press, 1970), pp. 136-37. Also, Charles Curran, *Contemporary Problems in Moral Theology* (Notre Dame, Ind.: Fides Publishers, 1970), pp. 144-45. For a discussion of Roman Catholic response in relationship to other Christians, see Gregory Baum, "Abortion: An Ecumenical Dilemma," in Thomas A. Shannon, ed., *Bioethics* (Ramsey, N.J.: Paulist Press, 1976), pp. 25-34. A recent exhaustive study of the Roman Catholic Church and Abortion is Susan T. Nicholson, *Abortion and the Roman Catholic Church* (Knoxville, Tenn.: JRE Studies in Religious Ethics, II, 1978).

12. A statement of this fact is provided in John T. Noonan, Jr., "An Almost Absolute Value in History," in John T. Noonan, Jr., ed., *The Morality of Abortion: Legal and Historical Perspectives* (Cambridge: Harvard University Press, 1970), pp. 1-59. For a discussion of the Christian values at stake in the problem of abortion see the chapter "Abortion and the Right to Life," in Harmon L. Smith, *Ethics and the New Medicine* (Nashville: Abingdon, 1970) pp. 17-54.

13. This point is made by James M. Gustafson in his writings on abortion. See, for instance, "A Protestant Ethical Approach," in John T. Noonan, ed., *The Morality of Abortion: Legal and Historical Perspectives* (Cambridge: Harvard University Press, 1970), p. 122.

14. For a discussion of the complex issues concerning the justification of war, see Paul Ramsey, *War and the Christian Conscience* (Durham: Duke University Press, 1961).

15. Stanley Hauerwas discusses this matter in the section on abortion in his book *A Community of Character: Toward a Constructive Christian Social Ethic* (Notre Dame, Ind.: University of Notre Dame Press, 1981). Though I come to different conclusions, I think he is right in his analysis.

16. Among the ramifications are the relationships to euthanasia. See Glanville Williams, "Euthanasia and Abortion," *University of Colorado Law Review*, 38 (1966).

17. Frederick Norwood demonstrates the single-minded concern of Methodism for the passage of the Volstead Act (the Eighteenth Amendment). See Frederick A. Norwood, *The Story of American Methodism* (Nashville: Abingdon, 1974), pp. 348-50.

Chapter 7

1. Thomas D. Kerenyi and Usha Chitkara, "Selective Birth in Twin Pregnancy with Discordancy for Down's Syndrome," *The New England Journal of Medicine,* 304 (June 18, 1981), 1525-27.

2. Raymond S. Duff and A. G. M. Campbell, "Moral and Ethical Dilemmas in the Special-Care Nursery," *The New England Journal of Medicine,* 289 (October 25, 1973), 890-94. A reprint of this article appears in Thomas A. Shannon, ed., *Bioethics* (Ramsey, N.J.: Paulist Press, 1976), pp. 75-85.

3. Shannon, ed., *Bioethics,* p. 78.

4. *Ibid.,* p. 83.

5. A careful ethical analysis of this well-known case is contributed by James M. Gustafson in an article entitled "Mongolism, Parental Desires, and the Right to Life," in Shannon, ed., *Bioethics,* pp. 95-121.

6. *Ibid.,* p. 80.

7. For a sensitive discussion of these issues, see John F. Dedek, *Contemporary Medical Ethics* (New York: Sheed & Ward, 1975), pp. 137-55.

8. Quoted in Shannon, ed., *Bioethics,* p. 96.

9. This case is reported in *Time* (July 6, 1981), 45.

10. Daniel Callahan, "Abortion: Some Ethical Issues," in David F. Walbert and J. Douglas Butler, eds., *Abortion, Society, and the Law* (Cleveland, Ohio: Case Western Reserve University Press, 1973), p. 101.

11. "Ethical Dilemmas in Current Obstetric and Newborn Care," *Report of the Sixty-Fifth Ross Conference on Pediatric Research* (Columbus, Ohio: Ross Laboratories, 1972), pp. 41-43.

BIBLIOGRAPHY

The working bibliography for this book is altogether too extensive to include in the volume. Still, I think it is important to provide suggestions for further reading. I have therefore established six categories of material: "Professions," "Ethics," "Christian Theology," "Abortion," "Severely Handicapped Children," and "Philosophical and Social Policy Issues."

These categories are arbitrary; many of the works could fit in several categories. I limited myself to twenty-five entries in each of the first three categories and ten each in the other three. The selection is personal in that I have cited those works which were particularly helpful in the development of this book. But also, I have attempted to provide a list of diverse representative works which will be of help to persons desiring further reading. The bibliography includes mainly recent works which are readily available.

I. *Professions*

Abel-Smith, Brian, and Stevens, Robert. *Lawyers and the Courts: A Sociological Study of the English Legal System, 1750–1965*. Cambridge: Harvard University Press, 1967.

Beauchamp, Tom L. and Bowie, Norman E., eds. *Ethical Theory and Business*. Englewood Cliffs, N. J.: Prentice-Hall, 1979.

Berlant, Jeffrey L. *Profession and Monopoly: A Study of Medicine in the United States and Great Britain*. Berkeley: University of California Press, 1975.

Bledstein, Burton J. *The Culture of Professionalism: The Middle Class and the Development of Higher Education in America.* New York: W. W. Norton & Co., 1978.

Bouwsma, William J. "Lawyers and Early Modern Culture." *American Historical Review* 78 (1973): 303-27.

Carlton, Wendy, *"In Our Professional Opinion . . .": The Primacy of Clinical Judgment Over Moral Choice.* Notre Dame, Ind.: Notre Dame University Press, 1978.

Carroll, Jackson W., and Wilson, Robert L. *Too Many Pastors?* New York: Pilgrim Press, 1980.

Cipolla, Carlo. "The Professions: The Long View." *Journal of European Economic History* 2 (1973): 37-52.

Donaldson, Thomas, and Werhane, Patricia, eds. *Ethical Issues in Business: A Philosophical Approach.* Englewood Cliffs, N. J.: Prentice-Hall, 1979.

Etzioni, Amitai. *The Semi-Professions and Their Organization.* New York: The Free Press, 1969.

Freidson, Eliot. *Professional Dominance: The Social Structure of Medical Care.* New York: Atherton Press, 1970.

Goode, William J.; Merton, Robert K.; and Huntington, Mary Jane. *The Professions in American Society.* New York: Russell Sage Foundation, 1957.

Layton, E. T., Jr. *The Revolt of the Engineers: Social Responsibility and the American Engineering Profession.* Cleveland, Ohio: Case Western Reserve University Press, 1971.

Lieberman, Jethro K. *Crisis at the Bar: Lawyers' Unethical Ethics and What to Do About It.* New York: W. W. Norton & Co., 1978.

Lynn, Kenneth S. *The Professions in America.* Boston: Beacon Press, 1963.

McGlothlin, William J. *The Professional Schools,* New York: The Center for Applied Research in Education, 1964.

McGuire, Joseph W. *Business and Society.* New York: McGraw-Hill Book Co., 1963.

Moore, Wilbert. *The Profession: Roles and Rules*. New York: Russell Sage Foundation, 1970.

Niebuhr, H. Richard. *The Purpose of the Church and Its Ministry: Reflections on the Aims of Theological Education*. New York: Harper & Brothers, 1956.

Parry, José, and Parry, Noel. *The Rise of the Medical Profession: A Study of Collective Social Mobility*. London: Helm, 1976.

Scott, Donald M. *From Office to Profession: The New England Ministry, 1750–1850*. Philadelphia: University of Pennsylvania Press, 1978.

Smith, Elliott Dunlap, ed. *Education for Professional Responsibility*. Pittsburgh: Carnegie Press, 1948.

Ulich, Robert. *Professional Education as a Humane Study*. New York: The Macmillan Co., 1956.

Vollmer, Howard M., and Mills, Donald L. *Professionalization*. Englewood Cliffs, N.J.: Prentice-Hall, 1966.

Young, James Harvey. *The Medical Messiahs*. Princeton: Princeton University Press, 1967.

II. *Ethics*

Beach, Waldo, and Niebuhr, H. Richard, eds. *Christian Ethics*. New York: Ronald Press, 1955.

Beauchamp, I., and Walters, L., eds. *Contemporary Issues in Bioethics*. Eucino: Dickenson Publishing Co., 1978.

Bernfield, Simon. *The Foundations of Jewish Ethics*. Melbourne, Fl.: Ktav Publishing House, 1968.

Bondi, Richard; Burrell, David B.; and Hauerwas, Stanley. *Truthfulness and Tragedy: Further Investigations in Christian Ethics*. Notre Dame, Ind.: University of Notre Dame Press, 1977.

Campbell, A. V. *Moral Dilemmas in Medicine*. Edinburgh: Churchill Livingstone, 1972.

Childress, James F. *Priorities in Biomedical Ethics*. Philadelphia: The Westminster Press, 1981.

Curran, Charles E. *Politics, Medicine, and Christian Ethics.* Philadelphia: Fortress Press, 1973.

Cutler, Donald R. *Updating Life and Death: Essays in Ethics and Medicine.* Boston: Beacon Press, 1969.

Dedek, John F. *Contemporary Medical Ethics.* New York: Sheed & Ward, 1975.

Goldman, Alan H. *The Moral Foundations of Professional Ethics.* Totowa, N. J.: Rowman & Littlefield, 1981.

Gustafson, James M. *Can Ethics Be Christian?* Chicago: University of Chicago Press, 1975.

_____. *The Contributions of Theology to Medical Ethics.* Milwaukee: Marquette University Press, 1975.

_____, et. al. *Moral Education: Five Lectures.* Cambridge: Harvard University Press, 1970.

_____. *Protestant and Roman Catholic Ethics: Prospects for Rapprochement.* Chicago: University of Chicago Press, 1978.

Hauerwas, Stanley, *Vision and Virtue: Essays in Christian Ethical Reflection.* Notre Dame, Ind.: Fides Publishers, 1974.

MacIntyre, Alisdair. *A Short History of Ethics.* New York: The Macmillan Co., 1966.

Maguire, Daniel C. *The Moral Choice.* Garden City, N. Y.: Doubleday & Co., 1978.

Niebuhr, H. Richard. *The Responsible Self.* New York: Harper & Row, 1963.

Purpel, David, and Ryan, Kevin, eds. *Moral Education: It Comes with the Territory.* Berkeley: McCutchan Publishing Corp., 1976.

Ramsey, Paul. *Ethics at the Edges of Life: Medical and Legal Intersections.* New Haven: Yale University Press, 1979.

_____. *The Patient as Person: Explorations in Medical Ethics.* New Haven: Yale University Press, 1970.

Reiser, Stanley Joel; Dyck, Arthur J.; Curran, William J., eds. *Ethics in Medicine: Historical Perspectives and Contemporary Concerns.* Cambridge, Mass.: The MIT Press, 1977.

Shannon, Thomas A., ed. *Bioethics*. Ramsey, N. J.: Paulist
   Press, 1976.

Smith, Harmon L. *Ethics and the New Medicine*. Nashville:
   Abingdon, 1970.

Veatch, Robert M. *Case Studies in Medical Ethics*. Cambridge:
   Harvard University Press, 1977.

III. *Christian Theology*

Bonino, José Míguez. *Doing Theology in a Revolutionary
   Situation*. Philadelphia: Fortress Press, 1975.

Campbell, Dennis M. *Authority and the Renewal of American
   Theology*. Philadelphia: Pilgrim Press, 1976.

Cobb, John B., Jr. *A Christian Natural Theology: Based on the
   Thought of Alfred North Whitehead*. Philadelphia: The
   Westminster Press, 1965.

Cone, James H. *A Black Theology of Liberation*. Philadelphia:
   J. B. Lippincott Co., 1970.

Cushman, Robert E. *Faith Seeking Understanding: Essays
   Theological and Critical*. Durham, N.C.: Duke University
   Press, 1981.

Dawson, Christopher. *The Formation of Christendom*. New
   York: Sheed & Ward, 1967.

Fuchs, Josef. *Natural Law: A Theological Investigation*. New
   York: Sheed & Ward, 1963.

Gilkey, Langdon. *Naming the Whirlwind: The Renewal of
   God-Language*. Indianapolis: Bobbs-Merrill, 1969.

Harned, David Baily. *Images for Self-Recognition: The Christian
   as Player, Sufferer, and Vandal*. New York: The Seabury
   Press, 1977.

Herzog, Frederick. *Liberation Theology: Liberation in Light of
   the Fourth Gospel*. New York: The Seabury Press, 1972.
   _____. *Justice Church: The New Function of the Church in
   North American Christianity*. Maryknoll, N. Y.: Orbis
   Books, 1980.

Kaufman, Gordon D. *Systematic Theology: A Historicist Perspective*. New York: Charles Scribners Sons, 1968.

Kelsey, David H. *The Uses of Scripture in Recent Theology*. Philadelphia: Fortress Press, 1975.

Langford, Thomas A. *In Search of Foundations*. Nashville: Abingdon, 1969.

_____. *Christian Wholeness*. Nashville: The Upper Room, 1978.

Niebuhr, H. Richard, *Radical Monotheism and Western Culture with Supplementary Essays*. London: Faber and Faber, 1960.

Oden, Thomas. *Agenda for Theology: Recovering Christian Roots*. New York: Harper & Row, 1979.

Ogden, Schubert M. *The Reality of God and Other Essays*. New York: Harper & Row, 1963.

Rahner, Karl. *Foundations of Christian Faith*. New York: The Seabury Press, 1977.

Saliers, Don E. *The Soul in Paraphrase: Prayer and the Religious Affections*. New York: The Seabury Press, 1980.

Shelp, Earl E., and Sunderland, Ronald, eds. *A Biblical Basis for Ministry*. Philadelphia: The Westminster Press, 1981.

Tracy, David. *Blessed Rage for Order: The New Pluralism in Theology*. New York: The Seabury Press, 1975.

Wainwright, Geoffrey. *Doxology: The Praise of God in Worship, Doctrine and Life*. New York: Oxford University Press, 1980.

Wood, Charles M. *The Formation of Christian Understanding: An Essay in Theological Hermeneutics*. Philadelphia: The Westminster Press, 1981.

Zaretsky, Irving I., and Leone, Mark P., eds. *Religious Movements in Contemporary America*. Princeton: Princeton University Press, 1974.

IV. *Abortion*

Callahan, Daniel. *Abortion: Law, Choice and Morality*. New York: The Macmillan Co., 1970.

Cohen, M.; Nagel, T.; and Scanlon, T., eds. *The Rights and Wrongs of Abortion*. Princeton: Princeton University Press, 1974.

Feinberg, Joel, ed. *The Problem of Abortion*. Belmont, Ca.: Wadsworth Publishing Co., 1973.

Lader, Lawrence. *Abortion II: Making the Revolution*. Boston: Beacon, Press, 1974.

Mohr, James C. *Abortion in America: The Origins and Evolution of National Policy, 1800–1900*. New York: Oxford University Press, 1978.

Nicholson, Susan T. *Abortion and the Roman Catholic Church*. Knoxville, Tenn.: JRE Studies in Religious Ethics, II, 1978.

Noonan, John. *A Private Choice: Abortion in America in the Seventies*. New York: The Free Press, 1979.

_____, ed. *The Morality of Abortion: Legal and Historical Perspectives*. Cambridge: Harvard University Press, 1970.

Shoemaker, Donald. *Abortion, the Bible and the Christian*. Grand Rapids: Baker Book House, 1977.

Walbert, David F., and Butler, J. Douglas, eds. *Abortion, Society, and the Law*. Cleveland, Ohio: Case Western Reserve University Press, 1973.

V. *Severely Handicapped Children*

Adams, Margaret. "Social Aspects of Medical Care for the Mentally Retarded." *New England Journal of Medicine* 286 (1972): 635-38.

Allen, David F., and Victoria S. *Ethical Issues in Mental Retardation*. Nashville: Abingdon, 1979.

Blum, Jeffrey M. *Pseudoscience and Mental Ability: The Origins and Fallacies of the I. Q. Controversy*. New York: Monthly Review Press, 1978.

Dedek, John F. *Human Life: Some Moral Issues*. New York: Sheed & Ward, 1972.

Ehrman, Lee; Omenn, Gilbert S.; and Caspari, Ernst, eds. *Genetics Environment and Behavior: Implications for Educational Policy*. New York: Academic Press, 1972.

Katz, Jay, and Capron, Alexander Morgan. *Catastrophic Diseases: Who Decides What? A Psychological and Legal Analysis of the Problems Posed by Hemodialysis and Organ Transplantation*. New York: Russell Sage Foundation, 1975.

Kelly, Sally, *et. al. Birth Defects: Risks and Consequences*. New York: Academic Press, 1976.

Ramsey, Paul. *The Ethics of Fetal Research*. New Haven: Yale University Press, 1975.

Smith, David, and Wilson, Ann Asper. *The Child with Down's Syndrome*. Philadelphia: W. B. Saunders Co., 1973.

Weber, Leonard J. *Who Shall Live? The Dilemma of Severely Handicapped Children and Its Meaning for Other Moral Issues*. Ramsey, N. J.: Paulist Press, 1976.

VI. *Philosophical and Social Policy Issues*

Blumberg, Paul. *Inequality in an Age of Decline*. New York: Oxford University Press, 1980.

Bok, Sissela. *Lying: Moral Choices in Public and Private Life*. New York: Pantheon Books, 1978.

Engelhardt, H. Tristram, Jr., and Daniel Callahan, eds. *Knowledge, Value and Belief*. Hastings-on-Hudson, N.Y.: The Hastings Center, 1978.

Jonas, Hans. *Philosophical Essays: From Ancient Creed to Technological Man*. Englewood Cliffs, N.J.: Prentice-Hall, 1974.

Peters, R. S. *Ethics and Education*. Glenview, Ill.: Scott, Foresman and Co., 1967.

Rice, Charles E. *Beyond Abortion: The Theory and Practice of the Secular State*. Chicago: Franciscan Herald Press, 1979.

Shea, William R., and King-Farlow, John, eds. *Values and the Quality of Life*. New York: Science History Publications, 1976.

St. John-Stevas, Norman. *Life, Death, and the Law*. New York: World Publishing Co., 1964.

Underwood, Kenneth W. *The Church, the University, and Social Policy*. Middletown, Conn.: Wesleyan University Press, 1969.

Wolff, Robert Paul. *The Poverty of Liberalism*. Boston: Beacon Press, 1968.

INDEX

171